MODERN CHINA

Orville Schell & Joseph Esherick

MODERN CHINA:

THE STORY OF A REVOLUTION

Alfred A. Knopf   New York

For the Committee of Concerned Asian Scholars—J.E.

For Ilka—O.S.

This Is a Borzoi Book Published by Alfred A. Knopf, Inc.

Trade Edition: ISBN: 0–394–82062–2
Library Edition: ISBN: 0–394–92062–7

Library of Congress Catalog Card Number: 75–181026

Library of Congress Cataloging in Publication Data

Schell, Orville. Modern China: the story of a revolution.

SUMMARY: Traces the history of China and its relationship with the West from the thirteenth-century visit of Marco Polo to the present day.

1. China—History—Juvenile literature. 1. China—History
I. Esherick, Joseph, joint author.
II. Title   DS736.S319   915.1'03'5   75–181026

Designed by Elliot Epstein
Manufactured in the United States of America

CONTENTS

ACKNOWLEDGEMENTS

Grateful acknowledgment is extended to the following for permission to reprint copyrighted material:

Columbia University Press: From "China as a Heap of Loose Sand" in SOURCES OF CHINESE TRADITION, edited by Wm. Theodore de Bary (1960).

Monthly Review Press: From CHINA SHAKES THE WORLD by Jack Belden. Copyright 1949 by Jack Belden.

Pantheon Books, a division of Random House, Inc.: From REPORT FROM A CHINESE VILLAGE by Jan Myrdal, translated by Maurice Michael. Copyright © 1965 by William Heinemann Ltd.

Paragon Book Reprint Corporation, for MODERN CHINESE HISTORY, SELECTED READINGS, by Harley Farnsworth MacNair, Copyright, 1970.

Random House, Inc.: From JOURNEY TO THE BEGINNING by Edgar Snow. Copyright © 1958 by Edgar Snow, and from THE OTHER SIDE OF THE RIVER by Edgar Snow. Copyright © 1962 by Edgar Snow.

William Morrow and Company, Inc.: From THUNDER OUT OF CHINA by Theodore White and Annalee Jacoby. Copyright 1946, © 1961 by William Sloane Associates, Inc. (reprinted with omissions).

Grateful acknowledgment is made for use of illustrations:

Brown Brothers, 4, 15 & 33

Magnum Photos; Photos by Rene Burri, 60, 64, 88 & 127; Photos by Henri-Cartier Bresson, 109, 119, 124, 128, 130 & 132; Photo by Robert Capa, 92 (courtesy of *Life Magazine*); Photos by Marc Riboud, 103, 115, 134 & 136

New-York Historical Society, 44

New York Public Library Picture Collection, 6, 12, 16, 18, 20, 24, 26, 27, 30, 37, 66, 96, 99 & 105

Photoworld, 56, 78, 107 & 121

Radio Times Hulton Picture Library, 23

Rapho Guillumette Pictures, Photo by Caio Carrubba, 139

Ullstein Bilderdienst, 40, 46, 50, 53, 72 & 75

The maps in this book are by Joseph P. Ascherl.

We wish to thank Shareen Brysac for doing the picture research for this book and Joanne Donoher for handling the permissions research.

MODERN CHINA

INTRODUCTION

If there is one character in the Chinese language that can tell us something about the ideals of traditional China, it is 安 (àn), which depicts a woman under the roof of a house. It might be translated "peace," but it means more than the mere absence of war and violence. It means harmony between all things: between man and the universe, between the poor and the rich, between husband and wife, between people and their government, between the emperor of China and heaven, and between China and the rest of the world. "Harmony" was the ideal of the Chinese philosopher Confucius, who lived five hundred years before Christ. For most of the period from about 206 B.C. to early in the twentieth century, the teachings of Confucius were a state creed—what we might call a religion—in China.

But these teachings were not a religion as those who live in the Western world think of a religion, with a personal God and a belief in an afterlife in heaven. Confucius was more concerned with human affairs than with gods, and he warned the Chinese people of ancient times, "We do not yet know how to serve men, how can we know about serving the spirits?"

Confucianism was a down-to-earth set of rules about how people should live together. Confucius regarded Chinese society, and the universe itself, as a pyramid in which everyone had his position and willingly fulfilled the duties attached to it. A son was supposed to be obedient to his father; the father, in turn, was supposed to respect the government official; the official would bow to his ruler, the emperor; and finally, the emperor would conduct himself in an upright and moral fashion obedient to the will of heaven. Every relationship in the society was clearly defined. "Let the ruler be ruler," said Confucius, "the minister be minister; let the father be father and the son be son."

This social pyramid endured as long as it did because Confucianism made it a virtue for a man to accept his given position in society. Few questioned the social order, and thus it could be maintained with a minimum use of force; the people of ancient China accepted the justice of their unequal ranks in society and behaved toward those above and below them in the proper Confucian manner. There is a poem in the ancient *Book of Odes* quoted by Confucius' disciple Mencius:

> *From East and West*
> *From North and South*
> *Came none who thought of disobedience.*

At the very top of the social pyramid was the Dragon Emperor, who ruled as absolute monarch. Below him, as in a giant layer cake, lay the various other strata of society: 1) scholars, government officials and landlord-gentry; 2) peasants and farmers; 3) craftsmen and laborers; and 4) merchants.

Scholars, government officials and landowners formed the upper class. The peasants, though the poorest, ranked just below because they labored in the fields, and it was considered honorable to till the soil that fed China's vast population. Craftsmen and laborers were the third rank, necessary but not highly esteemed. Lowest in the social order were merchants, considered vulgar, money-grubbing city people, and held in contempt by all those above them.

Clearly it was more prestigious in ancient China to be a scholar than to be a peasant, to be a craftsman than to be a lowly merchant; but according to Confucius, each class had a necessary function, and thus, whether inferior or superior, it was a rightful and worthy part of Chinese society. For over two thousand years China remained frozen in this pyramid.

Such a situation is difficult for Westerners to understand. In the United States, for example, there are few who do not hope to better themselves. People do not willingly accept second-class citizenship or resign themselves passively to poverty. Most Americans believe in equality, at least as an ideal. But in traditional China, equality was not an ideal. To the Chinese it seemed natural and just that some were at the top and some at the bottom. As Mencius said:

Some labor with their brains and some labor with their brawn. Those who labor with their brains govern others; those who labor with their brawn are governed by others. Those governed by others, feed them. Those who govern others are fed by them. This is a universal principle in the world.

The remarkable thing about traditional Chinese society was its ability to endure. The social order of China remained stable for two thousand years. Class revolution as we know it in the Western world was unheard of. In France, the king and aristocrats were guillotined during the French Revolution of 1789; in Russia, Communist rebels overthrew the czar and the Russian nobility during the revolution of 1917. Everywhere, class turned on class, the rich fought the poor, commoners fought nobles. But such a revolution was for centuries unknown in "changeless China."

Eventually, of course, China did change. Many explosive issues were hidden beneath the surface of the apparent "Confucian harmony," and they remained hidden until the peasants awoke and became conscious of the inequities and injustices of their society. This awakening finally led to a revolution that tore down the old order. The process was a slow one, but looking back, we can see that the seeds lay in the nature of traditional Chinese society itself. What, then, was it like to live in traditional China?

1
TRADITIONAL CHINA: A SOCIETY OF INEQUALITY

Peasant Life

Until the mid-nineteenth century, life for the peasant-farmers in the villages of China remained much as it had been for two thousand years. Travel was by river and canal, and most villages, with their mud or bamboo houses, were almost completely cut off from each other and from the cities. Narrow footpaths wound through the mountains and down into the valleys, following along the irrigation dikes that separated one rice paddy or green field from the next. In the rainy season, mud and potholes made these footpaths impassable; in the dry season, they were choked with dust. There were few roads, and no cars, buses or trains. It was along the muddy footpaths that the Chinese peasant walked to his local market town, trudging many miles with his produce on his back.

But such trips were rare, even for the lucky peasant with an oxcart, for few could afford to leave their fields untended even for a single day. And a peasant had precious little to sell at the market anyway, and little money to spend there except for the necessities of life—salt, cloth, and enough seed for planting. In addition, there were so many dialects of the Chinese language, and each small village was so isolated from the next, that a man traveling to the next county would have difficulty understanding the local people. The peasant-farmer of China built his life around his own village, and the floorless, stamped-earth hut where he was born, where he married, and where he died. The world outside his village must have seemed as remote as another planet.

Life in a Chinese village was hard and monotonous. Clusters of drab houses stood like small islands in the sea of surrounding fields. Whole families crowded into one or two dark rooms. In the winter, the paneless windows were boarded to retain animal heat, since in much of China the forests had long since been destroyed for fuel. Frequently chickens, pigs, and an ox would share the house in the cold winter months. Food was so scarce that dogs were rarely kept as pets, and often eaten. Here a man lived with his wife, several children, and perhaps his aging parents. From the time he awoke in the morning until he went to sleep at night, the peasant toiled in the fields to feed his family.

Pressing sugar cane in a typical Chinese mill.

These fields were small, patchwork plots scattered here and there at random. In China, no fields of corn or wheat stretched unbroken as far as the eyes could see; the land had

been divided and redivided over the centuries into a bewildering assortment of oddly-shaped plots, some no larger than a small room. Most peasant families owned less than two acres of land [or about half an acre per person.] The fields of the peasant who rented were often so far away from each other that he spent much of his time just walking to and from his crops, carrying his simple tools. A fortunate peasant might have an ox to help him plow the earth, but every field was planted and harvested by hand.

In the south of China, the peasants grew rice; in the north, they grew wheat for making oil cakes and noodles. But throughout China, harvests were meager, often insufficient to sustain life. During times of famine, millions of peasants ate nothing but bark and chaff and drank soup made from boiled leaves. One American missionary, traveling in Shansi province in the nineteenth century, made the following entry in his diary:

January 30th
Saw fourteen dead on the roadside. One had only a stocking on. His corpse was being dragged by a dog, so light it was. Two of the dead were women. They had had a burial, but it consisted only in turning their faces to the ground. The passers-by had dealt more kindly with one, for they had left her her clothes. A third corpse was a feast to a score of screaming crows and magpies . . . One old man beside whom I slowly climbed a hill said almost pathetically: "Our mules and donkeys are all eaten up. Our laborers are dead. What crime have we committed that God should punish us thus?"

If a peasant's land yielded a bowl of rice and a bowl of gruel a day for each member of his family after he had paid taxes, rent, and interest on loans, he was lucky. Vegetables were available only in summer, and meat was an unthinkable luxury. Even today Chinese farmers jokingly recall the times when they had to drink "white tea"—hot water—be-

cause they couldn't afford tea leaves. As one historian ob-
served, the peasantry of China was like a man standing up
to his neck in water: just a ripple would drown him.

Constantly threatened with starvation, the Chinese peasant had no one to fall back on but his family. Only in south
China, where people lived together in large clan organizations composed of every blood relation, rich and poor, could
a peasant expect any group assistance. There were no rural
cooperatives where a farmer could buy and sell at fair
prices, no credit unions offering low interest loans, no government welfare checks for the disabled or for those too old
to labor in the fields. The Chinese peasant was on his own.
The strength of his body was all that stood between him and
drought, famine and the bandits who lived in the hills and
plundered the valleys.

In Shansi province, in the northeast of China, a peasant
woman interviewed just after World War II described the
effects of a famine:

*There were three famine years in a row. The whole family
went out to beg for things to eat. In Chinchang city conditions were very bad. Many mothers threw newborn children
into the river. Many children wandered about on the streets
and could not find their mothers. We had to sell our eldest
daughter into slavery. She was then already fourteen.
Better move than to die, we thought. We sold what few
things we had. We took our patched quilt on a carrying pile
and set out for Changchih with our little boy in the basket
on the other end. We cried all the way from hunger. We
rested before a gate. Because the boy wept so bitterly a lady
came out. We stayed there three days. On the fourth morning the woman said that she wanted to buy the boy. We put
him on the k'ang [a platform of earthen brick warmed by
hot air from the stove]. He fell asleep. In the next room we
were paid five dollars. Then they drove us out. They were
afraid that when the boy woke up he would cry for his*

mother. My heart was so bitter, to sell one's own child was such a painful thing. We wept all day on the road.

The Rural Landlord-Gentry

Even if he survived the hardships of nature, the peasant still had to contend with the cruelty of his fellow men. To begin with, he was obliged to pay the government a back-breaking tax on any land he owned. This tax was collected for the government by the local gentry-landowners, who throughout China's history were the curse of the peasant.

But many Chinese peasants owned no land, or too little to see them through the long cold winters to the time of "spring hunger," when the last of the grain had to be saved to sow the next year's crop. If he should be forced to eat his seed grain, he would have to borrow seed from his landlord, for there was no one else to turn to. This was easily done, but the terms were severe. If the peasant couldn't pay the high price, he would have to seek a loan. But the only people with money to lend were the same landlord-gentry, and they could charge interest as high as 50 percent a month (over 600 percent a year!). A peasant who fell behind in his payments was forced to sell a cart, a work animal, his house, perhaps a child as a servant or concubine, and finally his land itself. The result was a desperate whirlpool of debt from which there was no escape. When everything was sold, the peasant had nothing left but his labor. His only alternatives were vagrancy, banditry or death.

In the 1940s, a peasant described the brutal exploitation practiced by the landlord-gentry in earlier times:

I grew up in the village of Feng chia tsa in Sui teh hsien. It was a small village. My family had always been farmers. We owned 15 mou and rented 30 mou [6 mou = 1 acre] from

Ma, the landlord. We had to pay 34 chin per mou [1 chin = 1.3 pounds] in rent. The landlord, Ma, had a money lending concern called Tsun teh. We did not borrow money from him, but we were not able to pay our rent. He took interest on it and interest on the interest. It was high rent. The years were not bad and the crops were middling good, but we were six mouths to feed in the family, and in the end our debt increased to 1,200 chin of grain. So then he took our 15 mou of land from us. I was twelve or thirteen years old then. There was no way we could get out of it. We could not get out of his clutches. The next year we rented the fields which had formerly been our own, and had to pay 30 chin per mou rental for them. Father said, "What can we do? The landowner is hard. He takes our land from us. But they have the money and power and there is no way out for us. We must bow to it." Father had no hope any longer. He did not dare talk with others in the village. If he had, he would have been suspected of stirring up mischief. Mother just wept. Having four children, it was hard for her to have lost those 15 mou. She kept saying, "Life is much worse now . . ."

The landlord, Ma, lived forty li away [about 17 miles]. So we did not see him often. But his agent, the manager of Tsun teh, his money-lending business, had a round and bearded face. He was called Ma Shou-chen. He collected rents and ran the money lending. He was not a nice man. He was always stiff and dignified. He never smiled. He never showed either anger or pleasure. He was just as suave and hard as a stone.

In their poverty, the peasants of China had almost no way to affect the decisions that controlled their destiny, for in China the government itself was staffed by landlord–gentry and represented their interests and not the interests of the peasant.

As they toiled in the fields the peasants sang:

I plough my ground and eat
I dig my well and drink;
For King or Emperor
What use have I?

So cut off was the average man from the affairs of state
that he knew nothing of his own government. As one old
peasant recalled:

We never saw any government officials, and I have no idea
when the dynasty went. At all events we never noticed any-
thing in our village of those revolutions. Everything stayed
the same. The farmer suffered just as much all the time.

In each of the cities and towns where the rich officials
and gentry resided, they collected taxes for the state, con-
scripted armies, owned most of the land and controlled
local politics. Some of them were extremely wealthy. They
owned houses in the city, and sent their sons to the provincial capitals and Peking to become scholars and officials. But
the majority were less impressive, had less education, and
their power and influence was local. Living in rural China,
however, they took great pains to distinguish themselves
from what they considered the coarseness of rural, or peasant life. They rode in palanquins (sedan chairs) and dressed
in long silk gowns decorated with fur and embroidery.
They scorned manual labor as the occupation of "small
men." Although some were educated, many more simply
made pretensions to learning, for in China education commanded great respect. As a status symbol, members of the
gentry allowed the nails on both little fingers to grow very
long to show that they worked with their minds, not with
their hands. Had not Confucius said, "It is the way of
heaven that the superior man attends to spiritual things and
not to his livelihood?"

In a typical rural community, the landlord-gentry made

A sedan chair, the characteristic mode of travel for a Chinese official. (1907)

up less than five percent of the population, but in many areas they owned more than half of the land, as well as many of the houses, draft animals and farm tools. Their homes, though less luxurious than the mansions of the rich city-dwellers, were large and well constructed. Invariably the houses were surrounded by high mortar walls, which served as both practical and symbolic barriers between themselves and the outside world.

Upon occasion, if the situation was bad enough in the countryside, the emperor or some high official might issue an edict curbing the exploitation of peasant by gentry. In 1679 Emperor Kang Hsi issued the following decree:

Lawless gentry and scholars who privately prepare flogging boards and sticks, in order to punish their tenants without authorization; and those who appropriate women of tenant families, making them their slaves and concubines, shall be deprived of their ranks and titles and punished for their offenses.

The emperor's intentions may have been good. Unfortunately the historical record contains few stories of gentry punished for their cruelty and selfishness.

In rural China, where want was a condition of life, the landlord-gentry lived in an oasis of plenty. They ate well all year long and always had fuel to heat their houses. All had servants, and many were rich enough to marry a second or third wife, or buy a concubine. Instead of working in the fields, their sons spent their time managing their estates or studying the Confucian classics. In short, the landlord-gentry were parasites, living off the labor of the poor. The only positive functions they served were to mobilize manpower and funds for such public projects as irrigation and road-building, and to act as informal judges to settle local quarrels. Terrified of going to court, the peasants willingly accepted the arbitration of the gentry.

The landlord also served as the local law enforcement agency. Through his connection with county and provincial officials, he could call in troops to crush rice riots, tax rebellions or the activities of bandit groups operating in the hills. Landowners were secure in the knowledge that imperial troops could always be called upon to restore order and protect their interests.

The landlord-gentry, then, acted as a self-appointed government in the villages of traditional China. They were an unofficial link between the two worlds of the country and the city, the peasant and the scholar, the rich and the poor, the people and the government. Among the peasants they were known as *kou t'ui-tzu,* the "feet of the dog." From inside the high walls of their rural bastions, the landlord-gentry regulated the economic, social and political life of the surrounding countryside.

Though the immense power of the landlord-gentry was backed up by police and soldiers, it was the acquiescence of the peasants to the Confucian system that finally assured order in the countryside. For no matter how miserable the lot of a peasant, he stood in awe before his landlord, a Confucian gentleman, who was rich, literate and had the blessing of the emperor, the Son of Heaven.

The Cities

Though the landlord-gentry were representatives of Confucian culture in rural China, it was in the cities that high Chinese civilization arose and flourished. Here the sons of the cultured elite studied the Confucian classics to prepare for government examinations, the gateway to officialdom. The cities were also centers of trade, where merchants amassed huge fortunes and became patrons of libraries, artists, poets and the scholarly academies of China.

Despite their role in cultural activities, the merchants of China were not highly esteemed, for commerce was traditionally considered a vulgar pastime. Many made pretensions to learning, and spent vast sums educating their sons to become Confucian gentlemen. Only in this way could they hope to raise their family status from its position at the bottom of the social hierarchy. In traditional China, wealth, though it could buy learning, was no substitute for learning.

Other merchants, of course, had no such aspirations, and simply reveled in their wealth. One enterprising Yang-chou salt merchant, determined to spend ten thousand taels (one tael = 37.8 grams) worth of silver in one day, climbed a tower and threw down heaps of gold foil, which, "carried by the wind, soon scattered amidst trees and grass, and could not be gathered again."

But the riches of the merchants existed side by side with the poverty of the city laborer. A French journalist described Canton in the early nineteenth century:

The main impression one brings back after having visited that city is of having wandered around in a vast sewer . . . All day long coolies make their way through the crowd, carrying a pole on their shoulders, at each end of which hang wooden vessels filled with feces. Foul stenches rise from aging heaps of refuse piled up on every corner. A filthy canal, full of all sorts of objects stuck in its stinking mud, winds its way through the city . . . The bridges span-

ning it have stairways, whose steps are crowded with hideous beggars harassing the many passers-by with their ceaseless wailing . . .

Scene in a school which was the privilege only of upper-class children.

In any event, whether a merchant squandered his money or spent it in an attempt to become a member of the learned elite, he rarely reinvested it, and thus he failed to become an agent of economic growth. Commerce in salt, grain, cloth, and many other items flourished in China, but modern industry did not develop until the nineteenth and twentieth centuries, when foreign invasion dragged China unwillingly into the world market system.

Because trade was despised, most men sought wealth

Chinese during the Manchu dynasty in their traditional pigtails at an open air bird market in Peking.

through ownership of land. Land and learning became contingent on each other, for without land from which to extract an income, a man could not find the leisure to spend his life in study and become truly learned, the ideal of peasant, merchant and gentry alike. Learning was an investment: through it one might acquire a government position and political power; through political power one could protect one's wealth and insure the future prestige of one's family. Land equaled wealth, wealth led to learning, and learning led to power and a position at the top of the social hierarchy as a scholar-official in the imperial government.

After passing the official examinations, the scholar-officials served their terms in distant parts of China, where they represented the emperor to the people, rather than representing the people to the emperor (sometimes they didn't even speak the local dialect). In their leisure time they practiced calligraphy, painted, wrote poetry and tried to cultivate that life of perfect harmony and gentility that was the ideal of every Confucian gentleman. They strove to be masters of culture, politics and human relations—what we might call Renaissance men—rather than specialists in any field. They were the high priests of Chinese culture, who produced the subtleties and refinement of a T'ang Dynasty poem, a Sung landscape painting, a Ming ceramic, or a Ch'ing encyclopedia. They created the Chinese culture, a civilization that has been equaled by few others in history. It was a magnificent creation, at which Western nations have marveled ever since their first contact with the Orient.

But no matter how beautiful a Ming ceramic or a Sung landscape, it had little significance for the vast majority of the Chinese people, though the social order that made such a refinement possible was built on their labor in the fields. One is finally moved to wonder how a society embracing such inequities could have proved as stable and enduring as it did.

Throughout Chinese history, of course, there have been peasant rebellions, and from earliest times peasants have regularly risen in anger and desperation to demand more food or land, lower rent, and fewer taxes. The activities of bandits, secret societies, and rebellious religious sects have long punctuated Chinese history. But by and large, such rebellions asked only for a new emperor or a new dynasty to restore virtue to the old way of doing things. The rebel leaders did not rise against the Confucian order itself. One did not ask the basic revolutionary questions: "Why must things be as they are?" "Why are men born unequal?" "Why must it be that some work while others do not?" Rather than calling for destruction of the system itself, they asked for a better place in it. Whenever they dared to hope for a better lot, they looked backward to the past rather than forward to a new vision of life. For what man can challenge the injustice of a traditional system before he is conscious of an alternative?

But in the middle of the nineteenth century, European vessels penetrated the south China coast. At last the Chinese people were forced to become aware that there were alternatives to the system and the way of looking at themselves and the world that they had accepted for so long.

2
MERCHANTS AND GUNS: WESTERN INVASION

The Western world—our world—first learned about China through Marco Polo, an Italian traveler who wandered through the cities and bazaars of central Asia and China in 1271, and brought back fantastic reports of the riches and spices of the Orient. He then wrote the *Description of the World,* a book that became tremendously popular in Europe, was translated into many languages, and for hundreds of years was the main source of European knowledge about Cathay, Polo's name for China. Such was the West's first impression of China.

Barbarians & Foreign Devils

But China's first impression of the West is a rather different one. Marco Polo played little part in history as seen through Chinese eyes. To them, the Western world really arrived in the sixteenth century, after the time of Columbus, when square-rigged sailing ships set out from the nations of Europe in hopes of bringing home Oriental teas, silks, and spices. Unlike Marco Polo, the sailors and captains of these ships which began to put in along the southern coast of China were fortune seekers, not at all interested in Chinese culture and society. All they wanted was profit, and they cared little how they got it. We shall see what impression such Westerners made on the Chinese.

The famous "Great Wall" of China.

In 1514, Portuguese sailing ships touched China's southern coast, the very first European ships to land there. By 1557, they had rented the southern port city of Macao from China, and from its harbor their vessels carried on a busy trade in silks and spices. The Chinese impression of these Portuguese sailors was not always a good one. The Chinese found the Europeans physically repugnant: they were big men with long noses, hairy chests, heavy beards, and they were sweaty and smelly after long months at sea. After being cooped up aboard ship, the sailors wanted only two things when they landed in China—wine and women. Naturally the restrained, Confucian Chinese, with their tea ceremonies and formal bows of politeness, found them coarse and unruly.

One early Chinese account of Westerners described them as follows:

Europe's people are all tall and white. Only those who live in the northeast, where it is very cold, are short and dwarfish. They have big noses and deep eyes. But their eyes are not of the same color, with brown, green and black being most frequent. They have heavy beards that go up to their temples and are wound around their jaws. Some of their beards are straight like those of the Chinese. Some are crooked and twisted like curly hairs. Some shave them off. Some leave them all on. Some cut off their beards but leave their mustaches. Some cut off their mustaches but leave their beards. They do what they wish. Whether old or young, all have beards. They let their hair grow two or three inches. But if it gets longer they cut it. They wear flat topped, tube like, narrow-brimmed hats of different heights, from four inches to over one foot. They are made of felt or silk. When they meet people they lift their hats as a sign of respect.

The Chinese scholar Hwuy-ung rendered a similar account:

They all look alike, though differing in height; some being very tall. My present idea of them is ugliness and stiff angular demeanor, perhaps due to ungainly garments . . . Their cheeks are white and hollow, though occasionally purple; their noses like sharp beaks, which we consider unfavorable. Some of them have thick tufts of hair, red and yellow, on their faces, making them look like monkeys. Their arms and ears do not reach the floor as they are depicted by us. Though sleepy looking, I think they have intelligence . . .

To the Chinese, these Europeans were "barbarians," or "foreign devils," without culture or learning, and no better than the Mongols who had invaded their country on horseback from the north. Indeed, "barbarian" was a term the Chinese applied to all foreigners.

What did these foreign ships carry in their holds to offer the Chinese? Very little. The Portuguese—and the Dutch, English, French, and American sailing ships that followed them in later centuries—took home teas, silks, and porcelain for the drawing rooms of Europe, but they had virtually nothing to offer China in exchange. Feeling that the Westerners were repugnant and sought only to drain China of her wealth, the emperor made most of China off-limits to such ships and sailors; they were permitted to drop anchor in only one port, Canton. In 1793, when the British sent an ambassador to the Manchu Emperor then ruling from Peking to protest this policy and negotiate better trade regulations, the Chinese emperor wrote a letter to King George III that illustrated China's feelings about the West very clearly:

You, O King, live beyond the confines of many seas, nevertheless, impelled by your humble desire to partake of the benefits of our civilizations, you have dispatched a mission . . . Your Envoy has crossed the seas and paid his respects at my Court on the anniversary of my birthday. To show your devotion, you have also sent offerings of your country's produce.

I have perused your [request]: the earnest terms in which it is couched reveal a respectful humility on your part, which is highly praiseworthy. In consideration of the fact that your Ambassador and his deputy have come a long way with your [request] and tribute, I have shown them high favor, and have allowed them to be introduced into my presence. To manifest my indulgence, I have entertained them at banquets and made them numerous gifts . . .

As to your entreaty to send one of your nationals to be accredited to my Celestial Court and to be in control of your country's trade with China, this request is contrary to all usage of my dynasty and cannot possibly be entertained.

The latter part of the emperor's letter, written in polite terms, gives a picture of his sense of the relative importance of China and of England. The emperor would not accept a British ambassador to his court because:

Europe consists of many other nations besides your own; if each and all demanded to be represented at our Court, how could we possibly consent? The thing is utterly impracticable. How can our dynasty alter its whole procedure and system of etiquette established for more than a century in order to meet your individual views? . . .

Swaying the wide world, I have but one aim in view, namely, to maintain a perfect governance and to fulfill the duties of the state: strange and costly objects do not interest me. If I have commanded that the tribute offerings sent by you, O King, are to be accepted, this was solely in consideration for the spirit which prompted you to dispatch them from afar. Our dynasty's majestic virtue has penetrated unto every country under heaven, and kings of all nations have offered their costly tribute by land and sea. As your Ambassador can see for himself, we possess all things. I set no value on objects strange or ingenious, and have no use for your country's manufactures. This then is my answer to your request . . .

The approach of the Emperor of China to his tent in China to receive the British Ambassador, the Earl of Macartney, in 1793. As the Chinese saw it, the paying of tribute and also the performance of the kowtow, the three kneelings and nine prostrations to which British and other Europeans objected, were acknowledgments of the Emperor's supreme power as a mediator between Heaven and Earth.

A street in Canton during the Manchu dynasty.

It becomes clear that though the Europeans might feel they needed tea and silk from China, there was really nothing from Europe that the Chinese felt they needed in return. Clearly, two different views of the world were coming into conflict. China had never known a civilization the equal of her own. She had always been the most advanced nation in Asia, and until the European Renaissance, the most advanced nation in the world. She called herself "the Middle Kingdom," meaning the center of the universe. Naturally, then, "barbarian" nations came to her in search of wealth and learning; naturally, too, they were expected to offer tribute to the emperor, presents that acknowledged him as the Son of Heaven and their overlord.

The British, of course, had a rather different view of things. Where the Chinese saw a hierarchy of nations, with China at the top, the British saw the equality of nations under law. The British expected trade to be open and free, as between equals. They were simply not about to consider themselves inferior to anyone, least of all to a quaint Chinese emperor who thought he was the Son of Heaven.

The Opium Wars

As the nineteenth century began, the Industrial Revolution was well under way in England. Her factories were the largest and busiest in the world, and her sailing ships ruled the oceans. Free trade was the heart of Britain's foreign policy, and it was not long before British merchants found a product to sell to a reluctant China in exchange for Chinese tea and silk. That product was opium, and it was opium that soon led to a real military confrontation between China and the West.

Opium proved to be the missing link in a trading "triangle" between England, India, and China. England shipped cotton fabric from her factories to India; British merchants in India grew opium for sale in China; and China was obliged to buy opium and sell tea and silk back to England. From an economic standpoint, this was all very neat and efficient, and certainly very profitable for the merchants dealing in the trade. The Chinese government, however, did not approve.

To the Chinese emperor, the opium trade seemed a double evil; the Son of Heaven had never wanted trade with the West in the first place, and now these Westerners were introducing a dangerous narcotic into China. Before the foreigners came, the people of China rarely smoked opium, but by the beginning of the nineteenth century, addiction to opium was ruining the lives of thousands of Chinese, many of them scholar-officials and soldiers. The army and government were becoming increasingly corrupt, while the trade in smuggled opium, which had been little more than 1,000 wooden chests, each weighing 133 pounds, in the 1700s, had by 1838 reached some 45,000 chests.

In alarm, the Chinese government took strong measures. In 1839, the emperor appointed a commissioner named Lin

An upper-class group of opium smokers in Hong Kong.

Tse-hsü, one of the most distinguished officials in the empire, to travel to Canton and halt the opium trade.

Upon arrival in Canton, Lin issued a proclamation to all foreigners denouncing their reckless search for profit, and declaring, "How dare you bring your country's vile opium into China, cheating and harming our people?"

But Commissioner Lin had a distressingly poor knowledge of the European nations, and even of China's trade with them. He believed, for example, that England's wealth and power derived not from her manufactures or her royal navy, but from her trade with China. Lin Tse-hsü somehow also held the odd notion that without tea and *rhubarb*, the Western countries could not survive a day! He never seemed to doubt Europe's utter dependence on China.

Believing this, Lin's approach to opium smuggling was logical: he cut off the trade, confiscated 20,000 chests of opium from the foreigner's warehouses in Canton, and burned six million dollars worth of the drug.

But his victory was short-lived, for King George and the British navy responded arrogantly with arms.

In 1839, the Opium War broke out, and during the four years from 1839 to 1842, the British easily defeated the Chinese time and again, bombarding up and down China's coastline. The Chinese, with their out-of-date weapons and a navy of sampans, were incapable of resisting the British. China's armies were weak, corrupt, and poorly organized. She had no choice but to accept peace on Britain's terms and sign her first treaty with a barbarian nation. It was a humiliation for China, and especially for the Manchu Dynasty then in power, which had been reassured only a few months earlier by one of their own officials that:

The English barbarians are an insignificant and detestable race, trusting to their strong ships and large guns; but the immense distance they have traversed will render the arrival of seasonal supplies impossible, and their soldiers, after a single defeat, being deprived of provisions, will become dispirited and lost ... Without, therefore, despising the enemy, we have no cause to fear them.

The attack and capture of Chuenpu, a scene from the Opium War, (1839–42)

The Treaty of Nanking, signed August 29, 1842, was the beginning of the first of many "unequal" treaties China was forced to sign with the West. China's people today regard the years between 1842 and 1943 as a century of oppression by what they now term Western imperialism. The Treaty of Nanking and those that followed meant that before long foreigners would be interfering in every aspect of China's political and economic life, and finally threatening China's very existence as an independent nation.

By the terms of the treaty, British sailing ships could now call and trade at five ports, instead of just one, along the Chinese coast. China also ceded to Britain the offshore island of Hong Kong, which became a British colony and has been a base for British trade and military operations in Asia ever since. Finally, the Nanking Treaty granted Great Britain the important right of extraterritoriality. This meant that a British subject accused of a crime in China would be tried in an English court of law. In theory, Britain had demanded extraterritoriality to protect her citizens from torture and possible death in Chinese prisons. But in fact, extraterritoriality was often used to protect foreigners who truly deserved punishment. If, for example, British sailors got into a drunken brawl with native Chinese, the Chinese courts were humiliatingly powerless to punish them. Instead, the sailors could scuttle back to their ship, where, as far as the Chinese could tell, they received little more than a reprimand.

It was the British who fought and defeated the Chinese to win these privileges, but other nations influential in the Far East—the United States, France, and subsequently all the lesser nations of Europe—acquired the same rights in similar treaties signed not long after 1842. The United States refrained from actually fighting the Chinese, but was quite willing to accept the same privileges that the British had won by force of arms. On July 3, 1843, China and the

United States signed the Treaty of Wang-hsia, almost an exact duplicate of the Treaty of Nanking.

The Western Invasion Continues

But the treaties solved nothing. The basic sources of conflict remained: China still refused to accept foreign nations as equals, and denied them the right to send permanent ambassadors to the court of the emperor at Peking. The number of ports open to Western commerce was still limited, while the European desire for greatly increased trade with China was still unfulfilled. Finally, foreigners were still excluded from the interior of China, where Western missionaries were eager to make Christian converts.

The British in particular remained intent on "opening" the interior of China, and in 1856 they finally found the excuse they needed to go to war again. A Chinese vessel, the *Arrow*, which had been registered in the new British colony of Hong Kong, and therefore flew the British flag, was boarded by Chinese navy officers and searched for smuggled goods. During the search, the Chinese officers lowered the British flag. England took this as an insult, and sufficient cause for war. And when at the same time, in the countryside of China, a French missionary was seized, tortured and executed for illegally entering a rebellious district, France, too, felt she had reason to go to war with China. And so, in 1856, the Arrow War began.

This war dragged on for four years, and once again Europe's navies bombarded the coast. Once again the Chinese were utterly defeated. The final humiliation came when a combined British and French force sacked the capital of Peking, drove out the Manchu emperor, and destroyed his elegant and luxurious Summer Palace. To the Chinese, Peking was a sacred city, the symbolic center of the universe;

A view of the Imperial City (Peking). (1910)

now it had been occupied by "barbarians," and the emperor had fled. It was the ultimate disgrace.

On their knees once again, the Chinese signed another treaty opening more ports to trade, agreeing to pay the Western powers more indemnity money, and allowing missionaries, anxious to convert the "heathen Chinese," to travel into the back country of China to preach.

The Chinese had never appreciated the activities of the Christian missionaries who came to the Orient to save souls. The Chinese did not want to be "saved"; satisfied with their own beliefs and their own forms of worship, they saw no need for the Western God. They were suspicious of the strange foreigners wandering about in their midst, and their suspicions led to hatred and conflict.

In 1870, a group of French nuns who ran an orphanage in the city of Tientsin offered a small sum to anyone who would bring them a child for instruction. The Chinese were convinced that this fee encouraged unscrupulous people to kidnap children and sell them to the nuns. Rumors circulated that the nuns were gouging out the eyes and hearts of the children, and eating them. The rumors were clearly false, but resentment of the foreigners was running so high, that on June 21, 1870, a mob descended on the orphanage. In panic, the French consul fired into the crowd, and what resulted came to be known as the Tientsin Massacre. The consul and twenty other foreigners were killed. A full-scale war was avoided on this occasion, but the Chinese were forced to send a mission of delegates to France to apologize. It was the first mission from China ever to visit Europe, and it was a humiliating way to begin.

Fourteen years later, in 1884, came the Sino-French War. This time the issue was control over the neighboring state of Vietnam, where the French wanted to set up a colony. Chinese land troops, armed with new Western rifles, were fairly successful against the foreigners, but the French destroyed virtually the entire Chinese navy as it lay at anchor in the harbor of Foochow, and they burned to the ground the Chinese shipyards that were beginning to build new, Western-type vessels. Just as in the Opium War and the Arrow War, this defeat by the French meant further loss of face for the Manchu government.

Repeated defeats at the hands of the Europeans were an embarrassment to China, but not nearly so shocking to their pride as the next war, the Sino-Japanese War of 1894–1895. The proud Chinese had always despised the Japanese, referring to them as "dwarfs." They regarded Japan as a small, tributary state owing ultimate allegiance to the emperor in Peking. Few Chinese realized that these hardy island people would soon threaten China's supremacy in the Eastern world.

While China had refused to change her ways when faced with the military superiority of the West, the Japanese Emperor Meiji had reformed and strengthened his country militarily, economically and politically. As a result, Japan had modern industries, a modern army and navy, and modern political and educational systems that included many innovations borrowed from the West. By 1894, Japan felt strong enough to challenge China for control of Korea— another country that had been dominated by China.

War with Japan was a rude shock to the Chinese people.

Their ground troops were quickly driven from Korea, while the efficient navy of the Japanese "dwarfs" ran circles around the far more numerous, but old-fashioned Chinese vessels. The Chinese cannons were rusted and often could neither be turned nor fired, while their ships were so poorly commanded by scholar-officials, skilled in classic literature but not in battle, that most of the navy was trapped in the Chinese harbor of Weihaiwei. Japanese forces captured China's own shore batteries, and turned the guns on the Chinese ships. Every ship in the fleet was either sunk or captured.

The Chinese government, it appears, had been more interested in pleasure palaces than national defense. The money that had been allotted for improving the navy had been diverted by corrupt officials toward rebuilding the Summer Palace in Peking, which had been destroyed by the British and French in 1860. While repairing the damage of one war, the Chinese government managed to lose another. In the words of one foreign observer, "China's collapse has been terrible, and the comical and tragical have dovetailed . . . in the most heartbreaking, sidebursting fashion."

As the nineteenth century drew to a close, foreigners seemed to have overrun China. Four times within half a century, they had defeated China in war. They had invaded the capital city and sacked the Summer Palace. Foreign missionaries were now traveling through the land preaching an alien religion, protected by the right of extraterritoriality; by 1907, the Protestants alone boasted 3,500 missionaries in China. Western merchants crisscrossed the nation in search of new markets for their goods, while Western gunboats traveled up and down the rivers of China to protect the merchants' interests. By 1900, the Americans and Europeans had begun to open mines, build railroads and steamship lines, operate factories and set up "concessions" or settlements in the major ports on the China Sea, and the major rivers of inland China. There, Western (not Chinese) law

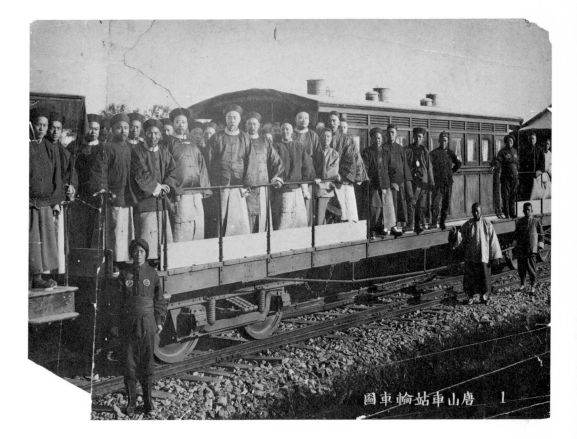

圖車輪站車山唐   1

was practiced, and Western (not Chinese) police kept the peace. One such "concession"—the international settlement at Shanghai—was virtually a European city on Chinese soil.

Gentry at the opening of the first railroad.

In order to appreciate the meaning of all this, we might imagine a similar situation in America today. Imagine the repeated defeat of the United States at the hands of an enemy and the sacking of Washington, D.C. Imagine a foreign enemy traveling freely through the nation preaching an alien doctrine. Try to envision hostile warships patrolling the Mississippi River, while enemy officials operate "concessions" in Boston, New York, and Los Angeles, and foreign engineers build railroads and factories across the land. Such an imaginary situation would be the equivalent of China's situation in the late nineteenth century.

The Chinese Reaction

This strange and unprecedented period of foreign attack and occupation created several different reactions among the Chinese people. Many tried to ignore the problem, refusing to believe that a real threat existed; but as the Western invasion continued, they began to fear that all that was China would be destroyed. Some attempted to imitate the West in order to protect themselves and preserve the imperial Chinese system. A third group of die-hard conservatives naively advocated the use of force to repel the hated foreigners, but China had no such force at her disposal. All these responses failed. There was only one practical alternative: if China was to save herself as a nation, she had first to destroy herself as a culture. The young, revolutionary nationalists who finally came to this conclusion sought to learn from the West in order to overthrow the emperor, the gentry—the entire Confucian system of government—and build a new China.

But why did so many Chinese try to ignore their problems? In part, it was because the rural areas of China had little contact with the Western intruders. There were no newspapers, radios or television sets to carry news of them to the isolated villages. But even more significant was the lack of a sense of unity or nationalism among the Chinese people. During the Opium War, many Chinese even served as coolies for the invading British army. To us, a man who assisted a foreign army in the invasion of his own nation would be a traitor. But can a man be a traitor to his nation when he has no idea what his "nation" is? That was the situation in China—the things people understood and valued were their villages, their families, and their customs. These were the things they were willing to fight for. In the Opium War, the people fought when their villages were threatened by foreigners foraging for food; they fought the missionaries in the Tientsin Massacre when they thought their children were threatened; and they fought when rail-

roads or telegraph lines violated their local customs or su-
perstitions.

But even among the educated gentry class, an individual's
horizon rarely extended beyond village and family, and if
these were safe, the faraway affairs of state—for China
was a very large country—did not concern him. You did not
think in terms of "saving the nation" from foreign invaders;
you thought of yourself as Wang, the peasant, from Shenping
village in the province of Honan, and as long as the Westerners left you alone, you ignored them.

The monk Régis-Evariste Huc, traveling in China during the nineteenth century, wrote of a vain attempt to stir
up a political conversation among some villagers at a small
country inn. "This apathy," he wrote,

*was really beginning to provoke us, when one of these
worthy Chinese, getting up from his seat, came and laid his
two hands on our shoulders in a manner quite paternal, and
said, smiling rather ironically, "Listen to me my friend!
Why should you trouble your heart and fatigue your head
by all these vain surmises? The Mandarins [Scholar-officials]
have to attend to affairs of State; they are paid for it. Let
them earn their money, then. But don't let us torment ourselves about what does not concern us. We should be great
fools to want to do political business for nothing."*

*"This is very conformable reason," cried the rest of the
company; and thereupon pointed out to us that our tea was
getting cold and our pipes were out . . .*

For most Chinese it took a long time to realize that these
"barbarians" from the West were different from the "barbarians" of the past—that they were not about to become
absorbed by the Chinese way of life, but would sooner or
later upset that Chinese tradition by introducing Western-
style commerce, religion, technology and ideas.

Not all Chinese ignored the West, however. Some, espe-

cially those who could read and write and those living along
the seacoast, who came into contact with the West, actually
attempted to imitate Westerners. The most interesting example of such an imitator was Hung Hsiu-ch'uan, who led a
revolt called the Taiping Rebellion. His bands of armed
peasant rebels raged over southern China from 1850 to 1864,
at the cost of twenty million lives.

Hung had been impressed with the military might of the
Westerners, and thought that their religion, Christianity,
was the source of their strength. So wherever his rebel
dynasty seized power, he replaced the Confucian classics
with the Christian Bible; he also introduced other Western
notions, such as the equality of all men, and of men and
women—an unheard-of idea in traditional Chinese society.
Overall, the Taiping rebel's ideas were a strange mixture of
traditional Chinese beliefs and new (though often poorly
understood) Christian concepts from the West.

Yet Hung and his Taiping rebels were not really typical
of those who sought to imitate the West. Few went as far as
he did, and among his band of followers there were probably
a great many more downtrodden, starving peasants rising
up against the gentry than there were converts to Hung's
pseudo-Christian egalitarianism. Hung was, in fact, a mystic
and a madman, believing himself to be the younger brother
of Jesus Christ.

Who were the other reformers? There were those who
looked at the Chinese army—most of whose soldiers were
still armed with swords, spears, and crossbows—and saw
that it needed modern, Western-style rifles and artillery.
China obviously needed a navy, not of sailboats, but of
steam-powered battleships and gunboats. She needed arse-
nals, shipyards, and steel mills, coal and iron mines, and
railroads. All these were indispensable if China was to defend herself against future invasions.

Yet China had none of these, and she had neither the scientists and engineers to help her build them, nor the schools

to train the technicians. If China was to pull herself up by the bootstraps, she would have to learn from the very Western nations that had humiliated her in war.

A scene in China in 1910 of a group of Westerners about to start for the Ming Tombs, twelve miles away. Each chair is carried by four boys.

The Failure of Reform

The Westerners, of course, were happy to tell the Chinese with proud self-confidence, "Learn from us." Many of them felt it to be their duty to help the Chinese "learn." As one United States minister to China stated, "Believing our civilization to be superior to theirs we should endeavor to elevate the Chinese to our standard." His good will mixed with condescension, and referring to China as "an ignorant pagan nation," he said, "It is simply pandering to the bigotry and self-conceit of the Chinese rulers, to treat them, under all circumstances and without any reservations, as independent and intelligent beings."

Now the Chinese, too, were a proud people. They were not inclined to humble themselves before "barbarians" who came to China with such attitudes. Even in defeat, most Chinese felt confident of China's spiritual superiority, and denied the need for major reform, insisting that if only a few corrupt officials were dismissed, the West could easily be defeated. As one high Manchu official put it, "The Empire is so great that one should not worry lest there be any lack of abilities therein . . . Why is it necessary to learn from the barbarians?"

But gradually the Chinese scholar-officials' resistance to reform weakened out of necessity. One of the first to realize that China would have to reform and modernize in order to survive was Commissioner Lin Tse-hsü, who had touched off the Opium War. After China's defeat and his own disgrace, he dared to state bluntly to the emperor: "After all, ships, guns and a water force are absolutely indispensable."

And his advice was taken. China did attempt to modernize militarily. In 1865, she built a new arsenal at Shanghai, and in 1866 a shipyard at Foochow; but the weapons produced by the arsenal were obsolete, and the shipyard was destroyed by the French in 1885. Some factories and mines were opened, usually with foreign assistance, but they were islands of change in a sea of official conservatism and corruption. The Chinese imperial government itself needed reform, and without that, real change was impossible. Chang Chih-tung, one early reformer, wrote angrily:

Among the capital and court officials those who can discuss new knowledge are silent and unheard. Why? Because they are impeded by all the erroneous ideas of all the absurd and narrow-minded scholars. This is pitiful and lamentable.

The shock that finally made reform seem possible came in 1895. Japan had defeated China in war, showing that it was possible for an Asian nation to strengthen itself by west-ernizing. Japan had made the reforms that the conservatives in China refused to make. It is reported that when the Chinese and Japanese negotiators met to sign the treaty that ended the Sino-Japanese War, the Japanese minister said, "Ten years ago at Tientsin I talked with you about reform. Why is it that up to now not a single thing has been changed or reformed?" To this the saddened representative from China could only reply, "Affairs in my country have been so confined by tradition."

The reformers finally got their chance. In 1898, the emperor of China, Kuang-hsü, was a young twenty-seven-year-old man, who reflected, "Westerners are all pursuing useful studies while we Chinese pursue useless studies. Thus the present situation is brought about."

And so the young emperor began the "Hundred Days of Reform." Between June 11 and September 21, 1898, he issued more than forty edicts on a vast range of subjects. He ordered the establishment of new schools and a new examination system modeled after the West; he encouraged students to go abroad to study; he sought to modernize the army, navy and police; he promoted industry, mining, commerce, and agriculture; he encouraged inventions and modern medicine. Finally, to insure that his orders were carried out, the emperor dismissed the most conservative officials in his government and abolished those honorary posts that served only to give jobs to old officials. There were many such useless posts in the administration, ranging from Supervisor of Eatables for Sacrifices, to Supervisor of Umbrella-Making for the Imperial Armory.

But this last move proved to be a dangerous one. Partly because their careers were threatened, and partly because they sincerely believed that the reformers were undermining tradition, the conservatives decided to fight back. They had a powerful ally in the elderly but crafty Empress Dowager, adopted mother of Emperor Kuang-hsü and mother of the previous emperor. From the time her own son ascended the

The Empress Dowager with Ladies of the Court.

throne in 1861 until Kuang-hsü came of age in 1889, she had dominated the imperial government. The list of her supporters was as long as her full name, which might modestly be translated: The Empress Dowager, Motherly and Auspicious, Orthodox and Heaven-Blessed, Prosperous and All-Nourishing, Glorious and Calm, Sedate and Sincere, Long-Lived and Respectful, Reverend and Worshipful, Illustrious and Exalted. Now this formidable woman was ready to regain power.

Once determined, she moved swiftly to secure the support of the army. She replaced the imperial guards with troops loyal to herself, and had the emperor seized and imprisoned for life in a small tower in the middle of a lake. The Empress Dowager drafted an edict in the emperor's name, turning over the reins of government to herself. The Hundred Days of Reform were over. The Chinese government had proved itself conservative and unwilling to modernize.

Within two years after the Hundred Days of Reform, the Chinese government shifted its position even more radically, toward violent resistance against all forms of Western influence. This policy change reflected the extreme peril of China at this time. Following the Japanese defeat of China in 1895, the European powers became convinced that China was falling apart, and they scrambled to pick up the pieces. They did not go so far as to establish colonies directly administered by Europeans, but they forced the Chinese government to recognize "spheres of influence," or parts of Chinese territory where the major powers had the exclusive right to all mines and railroads. In general, Russia's sphere was Manchuria; Britain controlled the Yangtze Valley in central China; France secured rights in southwest China, north of her colony in Vietnam; and Germany got the Shantung Peninsula in north China.

One radical Chinese reformer, K'ang Yu-wei, lamented, "The four barbarians are invading us and their attempted partition is gradually being carried out: China will soon perish."

The Boxer Rebellion

In response to this increasing foreign domination, there now arose a violently anti-foreign group, whc called themselves Boxers. The Boxers were a secret society dedicated to driving the foreigners out of China. They believed that through a magical form of Chinese boxing, they could make themselves invulnerable to Western guns. Forming themselves into small bands, they attacked foreigners wherever they found them. The heart of the Boxer movement lay in the new German "sphere of influence" in Shantung province, and among the first targets of Boxer attacks were German

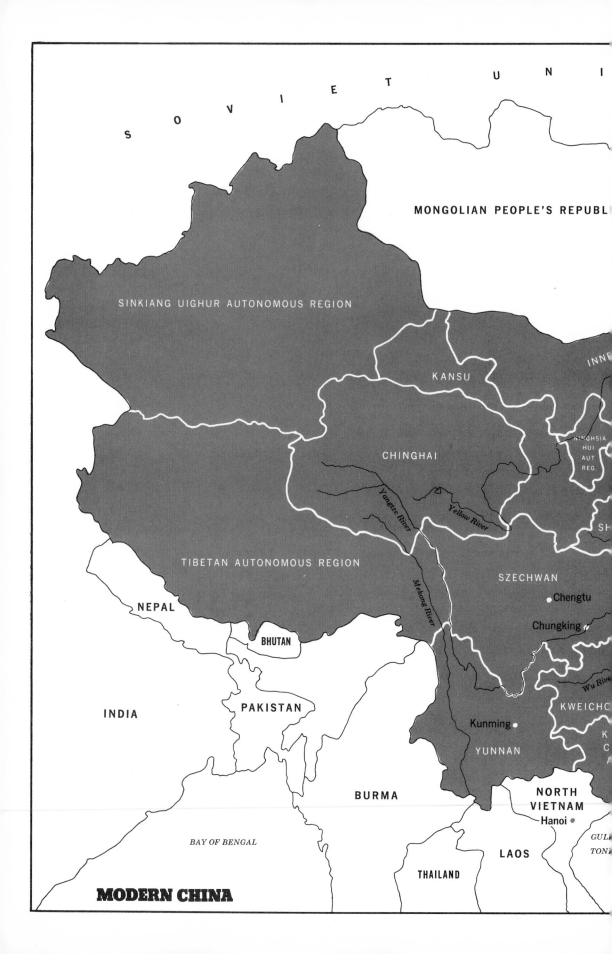

S O V I E T   U N I

S

MONGOLIAN PEOPLE'S REPUBL

SINKIANG UIGHUR AUTONOMOUS REGION

KANSU

INNE

CHINGHAI

NINGHSIA
HUI
AUT
REG

Yangtze River

Yellow River

SH

TIBETAN AUTONOMOUS REGION

Mekong River

SZECHWAN

• Chengtu

Chungking

NEPAL

BHUTAN

Wu River

INDIA

PAKISTAN

KWEICHO

K
C
A

Kunming •

YUNNAN

BURMA

NORTH
VIETNAM
Hanoi •

BAY OF BENGAL

GUL
TON

LAOS

THAILAND

MODERN CHINA

THE REAL TROUBLE WILL COME WITH THE "WAKE."

An English cartoon in Puck depicting the forces at work dismembering China during the Boxer Rebellion.

prospectors and railroad surveyors. But the more frequent and vulnerable targets were European and American missionaries and their Chinese converts in the countryside. In all, the Boxers killed some 242 foreigners and thousands of Chinese converts to Christianity in north China.

To the conservative Manchus, who had rejected reform and Westernization, the Boxers seemed to offer a way to rid China of the foreign menace. The Empress Dowager was persuaded to support the movement and join the effort to drive the foreigners out. The result was disastrous.

A combined force of 20,000 British, Japanese, Russian, American and German troops attacked the capital of Peking, and rescued several hundred foreigners and thousands of

Chinese who had been besieged in the foreign Legation Quarter. The Empress Dowager had to flee with her court to the countryside, traveling by oxcart in the humiliating disguise of a peasant woman.

The price China was to pay for the Boxer catastrophe was immense. Not only did she suffer destruction and looting at the hands of both Boxer and foreign troops, but the terms of the Boxer Protocol, signed on September 7, 1901 by China and eleven foreign powers, allowed the foreigners to station troops in Peking and along the railroad around the city, and required China to pay the staggering indemnity of $333,000,000.

Of the various Chinese responses to the West so far discussed, then, each was in its way a failure, yet at the same time each seemed to move China toward revolution. The young emperor's reforms were certainly more sophisticated than Hung Hsiu-ch'üan's imitation of Christianity, while the rise of the Boxers indicated that the apathy of the people could be overcome. After the Boxer disaster, even official conservatism weakened, and the Empress Dowager herself initiated reforms out of necessity.

But the time had passed for reform. People in China were beginning to demand more rapid and radical action to save the nation than the Manchu government was willing to allow. It became clear that the first obstacle to overcome was the reactionary Manchu regime itself, and one of the men who began that struggle against the Manchus was a young Chinese doctor named Sun Yat-sen.

3
CHINA'S FIRST REVOLUTION

Sun Yat-sen was a most un-Chinese sort of person. Born in 1866 near the city of Canton, home of many of the radicals of nineteenth-century China (including Hung Hsiu-ch'üan and K'ang Yu-wei), Sun left China at the age of thirteen. He traveled to Honolulu to study, and there was converted to Christianity. Returning to his village three years later, he treated the local gods with such disrespect that his neighbors drove him out. He went to Hong Kong to study medicine, and there earned his degree (thus he is often known as Dr. Sun Yat-sen), but when he moved to the Portuguese colony of Macao, colonial discrimination against Chinese there prevented him from practicing. This roused his nationalism, and he returned to Hong Kong, where he presented plans for reform to a prominent Chinese official. When he was ignored, Sun became convinced of the need for revolution.

In 1895, Sun Yat-sen engaged in his first plot against the Manchu government, but it was discovered and he had to flee to Japan, where he grew a mustache, wore Western clothes, and passed himself off as Japanese. From 1895 until 1911, he was not to return to China. Instead, living in foreign lands, he began to develop a philosophy of revolutionary nationalism. That such a man could be accepted as the spiritual leader of a revolutionary nationalist movement is amazing. Most of his education was Western, not Chinese; his typical dress was a Western-style suit; with his round face, short hair and mustache, he often appeared more

Japanese than Chinese; and he had spent almost all of his adult life either abroad or in the foreign colonies of Hong Kong and Macao. Yet this was the man who symbolized China's new nationalism.

The logic of Sun's revolutionary nationalism was relatively simple. He saw China on the verge of disintegration, about to be carved up and devoured by the Western imperialists. He blamed the Manchu emperors for China's weakness. Time and again they had led the nation to war and defeat. They had refused all reform, and now they did little more than collect taxes from the people and pay them to the foreigners as indemnity for past defeats. They were literally "selling out" the nation.

Sun felt humiliated as a Chinese before the power of the West. He wrote:

In the world today, what position do we occupy? Compared to the other peoples of the world we have the greatest population and our civilization is four thousand years old; we should therefore be advancing in the front rank with the nations of Europe and America. But the Chinese people have only family and clan solidarity; they do not have national spirit. Therefore, even though we have four hundred million people gathered together in one China, in reality they are just a heap of loose sand. Today we are the poorest and weakest nation in the world, and occupy the lowest position in international affairs. Other men are the carving knife and serving dish; we are the fish and the meat . . . As a consequence China is being transformed everywhere into a colony of the foreign powers.

The Manchus, said Sun, were responsible for all China's ills. Being an alien tribal group from Manchuria in the northernmost part of China, they were not interested in preserving the integrity of China as a nation. Yet Sun realized that it would not be enough simply to replace the Manchus with another dynasty. The monarchy itself had to be abolished, for a strong nation needed a strong government, and a strong government depended on the support of the people. To have the people behind it, a government had to represent its people —and so Sun believed China needed to become a republic.

For seventeen years, from 1894 until 1911, Sun worked from abroad to inspire revolution in China. He propagandized and raised funds abroad, and gradually his thinking and the thinking of other young Chinese like him began to make an impact, especially in the port cities where contact with different ideas and ways of life was greatest. The youth of China, especially the students and young army officers, made many attempts to start a revolution, but all were foiled and crushed.

But finally, on October 10, 1911, a revolution began that could not be crushed. An accidental bomb explosion brought the police to the headquarters of a group of young revolutionaries in the army in Wuchang. Finding themselves in a do or die position, the young rebels rose up and mobilized enough supporters to capture the city. Soon important people all over China—particularly army officers and liberal gentry whose hopes for reform had been frustrated—joined the revolutionary cause, and province after province began to declare itself independent of the Manchu government.

Sun Yat-sen learned of the revolution from a newspaper he saw in Denver, Colorado. He had played no role in planning the uprising, but once it had occurred he was considered the logical man to head the new government. Returning to China via Europe, he was sworn in as president of the Republic of China on January 1, 1912. The monarchy was gone at last. The head of the traditional hierarchy had been toppled, and the rest of the pyramid was beginning to crumble. China would never be the same again. "Unchanging China" had changed. And the young revolutionaries owed their loyalty not to the *government* of China, but to the *nation*.

Portrait of Sun Yat Sen and his military attachés in Shanghai after his trip to Nanking, where he was made President of the Republic of China in 1912.

Stillbirth of the Republic

Two months after he became president of the Republic, Sun Yat-sen promised the presidency to Yüan Shih-k'ai who helped to ease the Manchu emperor from the throne. Sun had realized that success was impossible without the support of Yüan Shih-k'ai, for he himself was little more than a spiritual leader of the revolution, with no real power: no army, no guns, no effective party organization. He needed Yüan and the army to complete the overthrow of the Manchus and the abolition of the monarchy, and so, in return for military assistance, he turned the presidency over to Yüan Shih-k'ai, who forced the Manchu emperor from the throne.

Yüan Shih-k'ai was a gifted administrator, but he was capable of great deceit. Like so many Chinese generals, he had adopted much that was modern, but beneath the surface a stubborn, conservative core remained, and he seemed to have a greater appreciation for flashy medals and colorful military uniforms than for the welfare of the Chinese people. Yüan was a man of no substance, a parody on himself. In 1911 he was the man in the middle, neither a revolutionary nor a conservative, both Westernized and a traditionalist. For many years he had served the Manchu Dynasty in both military and civil posts, but he had been dismissed in 1909 when the Manchu court became jealous of his considerable power over the army. The dismissal left him deeply resentful, and there can be little doubt that in 1911 he greeted the revolution against the Manchus with opportunistic pleasure.

But Yüan shared few of Sun Yat-sen's democratic, nationalist ideals. As an official under the Manchus, after the Boxer catastrophe he had favored gradual Westernizing reforms, and he himself had taken the lead in organizing China's first truly modern, Western-style army. But photographs of Yüan usually show a short, squat man dressed in the long embroidered gown of old-style Chinese officials. However modern his army was, he was still very much a man of traditional China. More than anything, however, Yüan was a practical military man who understood power and had devoted himself to attaining it.

And thus the revolution developed into a tragedy, for Yüan Shih-k'ai, the man with the power to carry out revolution, did not share the ideals of the revolutionaries. Once the Manchus had been disposed of, Yüan Shih-k'ai had no further use for Sun Yat-sen and his nationalism. Sun and his theories were totally foreign to Yüan's way of thinking. Yüan was interested in maintaining "law and order," not in establishing a republic or equalizing land ownership.

The situation came to a head when Yüan dismissed three provincial military commanders who were friendly to Sun and the Kuomintang Party, which had been set up in 1912 by Sun and several nationalist allies (literally it means National People's Party). The Kuomintang decided to resist the dismissals, and in 1913 began a "Second Revolution." It lasted but two months. Poorly armed and heavily outnumbered, the revolutionaries were quickly crushed by Yüan's troops, and Sun Yat-sen once again had to flee to exile in Japan. Sun, the "Father of the Republic of China," and the Kuomintang were back where they started from. We may speak to the two "faces" of the 1911 revolution: the power of Yüan and the ideals of Sun. But the only face that remained in 1913 was the face of Yüan Shih-k'ai, and he had it inscribed on so many coins of the Republic that you can still buy them in Hong Kong for a pittance.

The question arises: was life in China any different under Yüan Shih-k'ai, after a revolution, than it had been under the Manchu emperors? In many ways, no. For the peasants in the villages of China, life went on as before. They toiled in the fields while the government collected taxes and the gentry collected rent, just as they always had. The revolution of 1911 passed over their heads, and affected little more than their hairdos: they were no longer required to wear the long pigtails that the Manchus had prescribed for all Chinese.

Beyond this, nothing changed for them. If they had even heard that the Empire of China was now the Republic of China, and that China now had a president instead of an emperor, they probably would not have known what the words meant. And as long as it did not affect the next harvest, on which their lives depended, they probably would not have cared.

The revolution of 1911 was almost entirely a matter of coup d'états in the cities and provincial capitals. The people who believed in revolutionary nationalism were mostly city

Cutting off pigtails in the street of Nanking. The pigtail was a symbol of subjects of the Manchu dynasty, and cutting it off was a revolutionary act. (1912)

people: gentry, merchants, and intellectuals. There had been a series of confused, small battles over railway lines between major cities, but for the most part, local government and life in China remained unchanged.

As for the international scene, China as a nation continued to go downhill. Yüan needed money to support his armies, and the logical place for him to turn was abroad. In exchange for a loan of £25,000,000 (about $70 million) from a group of British, French, Russian, German and Japanese banks, he mortgaged the money from China's salt taxes, thus allowing the foreign nations to dominate the Salt Administration, which collected the taxes. And so foreigners gained control over one more aspect of China's economy.

One thing had changed, however: China was still by no means a democracy, but as president, Yüan Shih-k'ai would never be regarded with the same awe and respect that the Dragon Emperors of China had enjoyed. In traditional China, the emperor was the "Son of Heaven." The people believed in the legitimacy of his rule by inheritance, and respected his authority and obeyed his will unquestioningly. But Yüan Shih-k'ai was no "Son of Heaven," nor was he descended from past emperors. Therefore, he was not "legitimate" by tradition, and there was no guarantee that the people would respect his will as they had respected the will of emperors in the past.

Nor was Yüan "legitimate" in the eyes of the reformist avant-garde in the cities of China. Probably a man who could have promised them progress, or democracy, or freedom from imperialism, would have been "legitimate" in their eyes, at least. But Yüan Shih-k'ai's rule was based on only one thing—he controlled the army. That had made him president, and that in turn now put the government treasury in his hands. His philosophy of how to govern a country was simple: "People fear weapons and love gold."

Yet, in a strange way, he did seek to gain the love and respect of China's people. Rather than giving them a voice in their government, however, or actively working for what would benefit them, he looked to the past, to the respect that he thought would come to him if he was named emperor of China.

In the summer of 1915, with American support, a mock "election" was staged in which "representatives" from all the provinces of China miraculously cast a unanimous 1,993 votes in favor of a monarchy with Yüan as emperor. Yüan graciously accepted, and prepared for the enthronement. Through this curious combination of an election, as became a democracy, and an enthronement, as became Chinese tradition, Yüan Shih-k'ai hoped to make himself "legitimate" to everybody. But he had miscalculated the mood of China.

Yüan's own army officers were among the first to rebel. Many sent telegrams of protest, and some formed a "Protect the Nation" army to stop the enthronement. Several army commanders in the provinces declared their provinces independent. Under the strain of this crisis, Yüan abandoned his plans to become emperor, and not long after, suffering from nervous prostration, he died. On June 6, 1916, the era of emperors was gone forever.

The Warlords Carve Up China

For China, Yüan Shih-k'ai's death was a mixed blessing. She would never return to the old imperial rulers, but now she was without a leader of any kind. Army officers in the provinces and villages who had been loyal to Yüan Shih-k'ai, soon began to fend for themselves across the countryside. Throughout China, scores of army officers set themselves up as "warlords," each ruling over a given territory as dic-

Contrast between the homes of China's wealthy and poor is dramatically illustrated in this photograph.

tator. Poorer warlords lined up in cliques behind richer ones with more weapons, and fought petty wars for plunder and profit. During what came to be known as the "warlord era," the peasantry of China suffered immeasurably.

Time and again these warlords increased the taxes on land so they could feed and clothe their armies; tax rates jumped five or six times. Everything under the sun was taxed. In one city, for example, there was a tax on pork (the main meat in the Chinese diet) including a pig tax, a pig-slaughtering tax, pig-rearing tax, pig-selling tax, pig-inspecting tax, and pork surtax for educational expenses. There were taxes on prostitution: brothel license fee, brothel tax, lower-class prostitute singing tax, and license fee for prostitutes on call. Taxes on foods: flower tax, fruit tax, bean, sugar, and oil tax, chicken and duck tax, vegetable tax, onion and garlic tax, cockle, crab, and prawn tax, tea tax. And there were miscellaneous taxes: a firecracker tax, a tax on employees of fishing boats, and an opium-smoking lamp tax! The people of China were bled by taxes.

In addition, the people suffered by the absence of a strong national government. When natural disaster—famine or drought—struck, there was no national agency to transport food. The peasants fled before famine and after famine. An article in the *North China Herald* described one such desperate situation:

"Emaciated forms staggered along till they were unable to move another step, whereupon they simply dropped in their tracks. Parents were crawling along, leaving their starving children, too weary to move another step, crying piteously after them. Whole families were sitting desolately by the roadside, at the end of their resources and not knowing what to do next . . . The dead were better off than the living."

Whenever petty squabbles broke out between rival warlords, it was the peasantry that suffered most. Their rice fields were ruined, their houses were burned, and their meager supply of food was confiscated to feed the soldiers. Peasants left their villages and followed the armies as porters, while other peasants were forcibly drafted into the military. And at the taking of any town or city, the soldiers went on a rampage of looting. "Walking down the street I passed many soldiers in more or less ragged uniform," one observer reported,

"staggering along under their loads of watches, dollars, and other small but valuable loot they had taken. In every case they had their guns in position ready for use . . . They would step up to a man on the street, point their guns at him and demand his money. If he refused they threatened to fire . . . A number of soldiers went into the city temple, drew their guns on the shopkeepers, peddlers, customers, tea-drinkers, etc., and ordered that their dollars and banknotes be put into handkerchiefs and towels spread on a table. More than $600.00 was thereby netted."

This chaos and tragedy was made worse by the interference of foreign nations. To keep control of their "spheres of influence," Japan gave money and arms to the warlords in Manchuria, the British lent their aid to several warlords in the Yangtze Valley, and any number of private arms manufacturers from abroad peddled their weapons to warlords across the country.

For almost fifteen years, the warlords ravaged each other and China in a dizzying succession of meaningless battles. But all shared one ultimate aspiration, and that was the capture of Peking. The warlord who controlled the capital city could collect foreign customs revenues and salt taxes, as well as arrange loans from abroad, putting up the national treasury in one form or another as security. With so much at stake, competing warlords shifted around Peking; virtually every year saw a new "government" in power. For those who loved the Chinese nation, it was tragic. As one Chinese intellectual wrote,

In all the civil wars, the rifles and field guns come from abroad. The bullets and shells come from abroad. Bombs

and powder and hardware all come from abroad. The money comes from abroad. It has gone so far that in recent years the flour and military provisions come from abroad. Only the blood and flesh of our dead countrymen who kill one another on the battlefields are Chinese.

4
STUDENT PROTEST
AND THE BIRTH OF
CHINESE COMMUNISM

Protest against injustice seems to come naturally to the young. It was the students and intellectuals who first raised their voices during the warlord era in China. In 1919, news of a "deal" between a warlord Peking government and foreign powers sparked the first fiery student protests. At issue initially was Shantung province. Shantung, the home of Confucius, had been a German "sphere of influence," but as World War I broke out, Japan declared war on Germany and quickly occupied Shantung. In 1917, China, too, declared war on Germany, and sent 200,000 laborers to France to support the Allies. China's hopes were obvious: she thought that by joining the Allies, she might be granted control of Shantung at the post-war peace conference.

Unfortunately, Great Britain, France and Italy supported the acquisitive designs of Japan, and the latest warlord to be installed in Peking secretly agreed to relinquish Shantung in return for Japanese money to support his armies against his competitors. His complicity with the Japanese became known during the course of the Versailles Peace Conference, and when the news reached Peking, the students of China rose in protest. Truly the warlords were selling out the country, province by province. Everywhere students painted slogans on walls and buildings. DON'T FORGET OUR NATIONAL HUMILIATION, read one. STRUGGLE FOR SOVEREIGNTY—THROW OUT THE WARLORD TRAITORS, read another. Stores and shops were inscribed with signs that urged merchants to BOYCOTT FOREIGN GOODS.

On May 4, 1919, thousands of students from the colleges and universities in Peking gathered in a massive demonstration. Their nationalism was passionate. "The loss of Shantung means the destruction of the integrity of China's territory," they cried.

We earnestly hope that the whole nation will rise and hold citizens' meetings to strive to secure our sovereignty in foreign affairs and to get rid of the traitors at home. This is the last chance for China in her life and death struggle. Today we swear two solemn oaths with all our fellow countrymen: (1) China's territory may be conquered, but it cannot be given away; (2) the Chinese people may be massacred, but they will not surrender. Our country is about to be annihilated. Up, brethren!"

At first the demonstrators marched peacefully to the quarters of the foreign embassies in Peking, but when they were denied entrance, and then set upon by government troops and police, the students marched on the home of the "traitor" who had ceded Shantung to the Japanese. The crowd forced their way in, sacked the house, and on discovering the Chinese ambassador to Japan (who had actually signed the agreement), beat him senseless.

The student demonstration, which came to be called the May 4th Movement, had repurcussions long afterward. Throughout the nation, students followed the lead of their comrades in Peking, demonstrating and forcing the closing of all the major universities.

But the movement did not stop here. For the first time in Chinese history, a massive effort was made to organize resistance beyond the intellectual community. Merchants boycotted Japanese goods. In Shanghai, clerks and factory workers organized. Students spoke from street corners and distributed leaflets. In a matter of weeks, a massive popular movement was voicing its anger in all the major cities of China: the government must not sign the Versailles Treaty; the three officials responsible for the agreement with Japan must go. A rash of strikes spread across the country, with the desired effect—on June 10 the warlord Peking government, which had titular control over foreign affairs, but no organized support throughout China, dismissed the guilty officials; and on June 28, the Chinese delegation in Versailles refused to sign the treaty. China's first mass movement had won its first victory.

But by now the May 4th Movement had grown into something broader than concern over Shantung and the Versailles Peace Treaty. It was developing into a serious critique of traditional Chinese culture. Now, the students said, there could be no compromise with the past.

Hundreds of new underground magazines and periodicals sprang up to introduce new ideas, with titles like *Young China, New Tide, The New Woman, Save The Nation* and *New Youth*. It was in these months that Mao Tse-tung became active in a small group in the central province of Hunan called the New People's Study Society, and editor of an underground student publication *The Hsiang River Review*.

Born into a fairly well-to-do peasant family in Shaoshan village, Hunan Province in 1893, Mao was as yet unknown. But like so many other young men and women of his generation, the May 4th Movement was to play a crucial role in making him politically conscious, and aware of China's ailing condition. As the young people surveyed the situation, they began to realize that China would have no future unless she could overthrow her past traditions.

Confucian virtues began to come under heavy attack. The May 4th intellectuals pointed to the words of a traditional scholar who had written: "Because filial piety and fraternal duty are virtues of obedience, those who possess these

Old family portrait showing Mao Tse Tung (right) with his family in the province of Hunan.

virtues will not offend their superiors, and there will be of course no rebellion." One student's answer was, "The effect of the idea of filial piety has been to turn China into a big factory for the manufacturing of obedient subjects."

Confucian ethics, the students said, stifled protest, encouraged the unquestioning obedience of subjects to rulers, women to men, students to teachers, and young to old—while the old men, the rulers, the warlords led China to its sorry state. Now the young called for new values: individualism, nationalism, and finally communism, to forge a modern China.

Ch'en Tu-hsiu, a leader of the May 4th Movement who later became one of the founders of the Chinese Communist Party, wrote in *New Youth:*

Our ideal society is honest, progressive, positive, free, equalitarian, creative, beautiful, good, peaceful, cooperative, toilsome, but happy for the many. We look for the world that is false, conservative, negative, restricted, inequitable, hidebound, ugly, evil, war-torn, cruel, indolent, miserable for the many and felicitous for the few, to crumble until it disappears from sight.

I hope that those of you who are young will be self-conscious and that you will struggle . . . Why do I think you should struggle? Because it is necessary for you to use all the intelligence that you have to get rid of those who are decaying, who have lost their youth.

The 1920s saw the entire traditional social system of China called into question. Although for the moment the effects of the May 4th Movement were most felt in the cities, it was clear that if the movement spread throughout China, sons would be defying their fathers, students questioning their teachers, and peasants rising up against their landlords. The May 4th Movement had not only planted the seeds of political revolution, but of a complete social and cultural upheaval.

If the movement was united in opposing the old culture, however, it was far from agreed on the goals and ethics to put in its place. The situation in China was typical of any age of intellectual ferment—the evil under attack was at first clearer than the good that was sought. In general, however, Chinese revolutionary thinking gravitated in one of three directions: toward Western individualism, Russian communism, or the nationalism of Sun Yat-sen and his Kuomintang Party.

To the younger intellectuals, Western individualism had a particularly strong appeal. Loosely, it meant the right of men to live their own lives; it meant youth would be freed from the restrictions of family and of the past. To a young man, Western individualism might mean marrying the woman *he* chose rather than one selected by his parents. To a woman, it might mean no more foot binding, a terrible crippling practice to which young women were subjected in

Footbinding was one of the customs objected to by Westerners. Yet some of the Chinese said that to them it seemed less uncomfortable to bind a foot tightly, as can be seen in the center figure in this photograph, than to bind a body tightly, as in a Western corset.

the belief that tiny feet were beautiful. To young writers and journalists, Western individualism meant freedom of speech and expression. And to students in general, individualism meant the right to think and expound their ideas as they pleased, and to criticize the Confucian classics and authoritarian teachers.

Among the intellectuals and young of China, Western

individualism was extremely popular. But at this moment in Chinese history, the fact remained that to live the free, individualist's life was basically selfish. Suppose the individual did have his rights—would this overthrow the warlords with their weapons? Would a few intellectuals publishing radical papers drive out the foreign imperialist nations? No, if China was to be saved from the twin evils of warlords and foreign manipulation, individuals would have to subordinate themselves in a national struggle. And this realization led many intellectuals toward communism.

Chinese Communism

To us it might seem strange that the May 4th Movement, which began as a nationalistic movement proclaiming China's independence, should gravitate toward communism. Americans have traditionally tended to see communism as an international movement directed by Moscow, and as a threat to the independence of any nation. However, the history of communism in Asia does not bear this out. There, communism and nationalism came together in their opposition to Western economic and political interference in Chinese affairs. Karl Marx had above all been concerned with the prospects for a revolution of workers against capitalists in nineteenth-century Europe. But Lenin, writing in the twentieth century, added a new element to Marx's analysis. He felt that the peoples of Africa and Asia were being exploited. He pointed to the extensive Western control of railways, mines and factories in Africa and Asia, and said that the workers of Europe and the peoples of all the underdeveloped nations must combine to overthrow the capitalist-imperialist oppressors. This appealed to many Chinese intellectuals, anxious to free their country from Western control and interference. And when, after the Russian Revolution of 1917, the Soviet Union took the unprecedented step of renouncing the old czarist government's interests in Manchuria, the northernmost section of China, the Chinese were impressed and grateful.

But communism offered more than anti-imperialism; it also offered an explanation of the evils of China's traditional culture. Viewed from the communist perspective, Confucianism was an ideology which the ruling landlord-official class could use to suppress the peasants and workers, by teaching them loyalty and filial devotion to "superiors." In the words of one famous Chinese writer, Lu Hsün:

Chinese culture is a culture of serving one's masters, who are triumphant at the cost of the misery of the multitude. Those who praise Chinese culture, whether they be Chinese or foreigners, conceive themselves as belonging to the ruling class.

Actually, the number of Chinese intellectuals who joined the Communist Party in 1920 was not very great. The First Communist Party Congress, which met in Shanghai in July, 1921, was attended by only twelve people, representing a total membership of fifty-seven. But these twelve were virtually all intellectuals, and two had been in the forefront of the May 4th rebellion, Ch'en Tu-hsiu, formerly Dean of the School of Letters at Peking University, and Li Ta-chao, Chief Librarian of the University. Also among the group was Mao Tse-tung, then a young library assistant to Li Ta-chao. These twelve, acting with the help of advisors from the Soviet Union, were the seed from which the Chinese Communist Party would eventually grow.

Sun Yat-sen's Kuomintang Party

At the same time, interest in another party had reawakened. This was Sun Yat-sen's Kuomintang Party, originally set up in 1912 after the fall of the Manchu dynasty.

Sun had been in Shanghai during the May 4th Movement, and had recognized the Movement as a significant outpouring of popular nationalist sentiment. He began to reorganize his now-defunct Kuomintang Party, and in 1920 he returned with some of his supporters to Canton, just north of Hong Kong in the southern province of Kwangtung. Here he tried to work with the local warlord, and for two years, he made considerable progress. The Kuomintang seemed on the verge of gaining control of the entire province of Kwangtung (long known for its revolutionary sentiments) when the treachery of warlord politics struck again—Sun's warlord ally, Ch'en Chiung-ming, turned on him in the ever-changing kaleidoscope of warlord power politics. With Ch'en against him, he was left without any armed support, and in 1923 he was forced to flee to Shanghai.

In the early 1920s, then, Sun found himself in a very difficult situation. In the aftermath of the May 4th Movement, nationalist sentiment was growing in cities throughout China. Membership in the new Kuomintang was increasing rapidly. The anti-imperialist labor movement was growing. In 1922, a seaman's strike crippled foreign shipping in Hong Kong and Canton. But still Sun and his fellow nationalists had no power; military power remained in the hands of the warlords and the foreign nations.

Twice Sun had attempted alliances with the warlords and twice he had been betrayed. So now he would look abroad, but it would not be the West that would offer him encouragement. He wrote:

We have lost hope of help from America, England, France or any other of the great powers. The only country that shows any signs of helping us in the south is the Soviet Government of Russia.

For their part, the Russians saw in Sun Yat-sen and the Kuomintang a force capable of leading the anti-imperialist struggle in China. In January, 1923, they signed an agreement with Sun promising both arms and advisors, in exchange for which he was to allow members of the Chinese Communist Party to join the Kuomintang. Sun himself was not a Communist. He did not believe in the value of class warfare, which he thought would only divide and weaken the nation. He also thought more highly of certain aspects of Confucian culture than did the Communists. But on the crucial issue—how to drive out the warlords and foreign powers—Sun and the Communists were in complete agreement. Sun had already codified his ideas in the Three People's Principles (*San min chu-i*) : nationalism (expel the foreigners and unite the country) ; democracy (Sun's notion of people's rights and ultimate democratic participation after a period of political "tutelage") ; and people's livelihood (the vaguest of Sun's Three Principles, which had an egalitarian socialist import to it).

By November, 1923, the political maneuverings of the warlords had come a complete circle around, enabling Sun to return to Canton, where he still had considerable support. This time he returned with Russian advisors, and went about the task of setting up a modern local government and an all-important military academy to train his own officer corps and free him from the need for warlord alliances. Whampoa Military Academy was headed by a young officer named Chiang Kai-shek, with the Soviet General Vassili K. Bluecher as his Chief-of-Staff. An able, young, French-educated officer, Chou En-lai, became Chiang's political commissar. With these men, Sun hoped to build a strong independent army with which to unify China.

Then, on March 12, 1925, just as his dreams for a strong, unified China seemed within reach, Sun Yat-sen died. With his death, the leadership of the Kuomintang passed to his loyal military assistant, Chiang Kai-shek. Though not the oldest or the most experienced Kuomintang leader, Chiang had been close to Sun. It was Chiang who, in 1923, had traveled to the Soviet Union to study Russia's Red Army, and as head of the Whampoa Military Academy, had helped supervise the organization of the Kuomintang's own army.

Chiang's Kuomintang

After his trip, however, Chiang had returned suspicious of Russia's motives in supporting the Kuomintang. He feared that Russia, too, would become just another imperialist power in China. Furthermore, like Sun, he did not wholly reject Confucianism, believing it to be part of China's "national essence." As a result, when he took over from Sun, tension between the Nationalist (Kuomintang) and Communist factions became unavoidable. Still, the fact remained that the task then facing the Kuomintang was the defeat of the warlords, and the military expert Chiang Kai-shek seemed to hold out the only possibility of unification.

In July, 1926, Chiang Kai-shek launched a "Northern Expedition," sweeping up from Canton with his army to drive the warlords from China. They were preceded by propaganda teams of idealistic young Communists, urging the people to help the cause by acting as scouts and porters, and by providing food and transport. In some regions of central China, Communist agitators (including Mao Tse-tung) called for more radical tactics, urging the peasants to make class war against the gentry as well as the warlords.

The northward march of the Kuomintang armies was supported by general strikes and demonstrations of workers in many of the major cities and foreign concessions. In the face of a tremendous show of popular enthusiasm for the nationalist cause, many of the warlords gave up without a fight. Some thirty-four warlords had joined the Kuomintang forces by the time Chiang reached the Yangtze River in November, 1926. In effect, Chiang had incorporated the warlords instead of defeating them. The new unity was illusory.

General Chiang Kai-shek, commanding officer of the Chinese army with two of his guards at the Gate of the Ming Tombs in Nanking, 1927.

Chiang Kai-shek now had the territory and military power to enable him to be a good deal more independent of his Communist allies, so he simply ignored the Communists and set up his own government in Nanking. The situation was similar to that in the 1911 revolution, when Yüan had taken over and become dictator; Chiang Kai-shek was on the way to becoming a warlord himself, and the Kuomintang found itself guided not by the ideals of Sun Yat-sen, but by the power of Chiang Kai-shek. It was becoming increasingly obvious that little had changed—that Chiang would rule not by ideas and by mobilizing the common man to his cause, but through manipulation of warlord factions and brute force.

During the early months of 1927, Chiang picked his moves carefully. The Communists were still potent among the city laborers and could be useful. In January, for example, they stimulated massive demonstrations that seized the foreign concessions of Hankow and Kiukiang along the Yangtze River, and eventually returned them to Chinese rule. In 1926 alone, they succeeded in organizing some 535 strikes. Such radical mobs made the foreigners interested in China all the more willing to deal with Chiang Kai-shek, who, though a sincere Chinese nationalist, was at least less radical than the Communists.

When a Communist-led workers' movement in Shanghai seized the Chinese section of the city, both foreigners and native Chinese business and commercial interests were near hysteria. The foreign press screamed "mad dog of Bolshevism," predicting the imminent destruction of civilization and falsely reporting that Chinese women were demonstrating naked in the streets as evidence of "the pernicious influence of Russian Communism." Now, some foreigners began to see in Chiang Kai-shek a possible alternative to communism in China, which they feared would not only end the warlord period, but destroy their privileged positions in China. They were joined by rich Chinese who had begun to fear the loss of their huge land holdings if Communist influence grew.

And Chiang Kai-shek was their man. He began to negotiate with bankers, capitalists and members of Shanghai's underworld. Precisely what sort of a deal was made is not clear, but Chiang reportedly received a total of 25 million Shanghai dollars, with a 30 million dollar loan to the Nanking government to come two weeks later. In exchange for this financial support, Chiang agreed to use his army to liquidate the Communists. By doing so, in a single stroke, he shifted his loyalty from the mass movement of workers and peasants organized by the Communists, to the small elite of wealthy businessmen in the coastal cities. It was a decision which cast the die of Chinese history for the next twenty years.

On April 12, 1927, a blood bath began. Chiang's troops, with the help of the most powerful underworld gangs in Shanghai, launched a brutal suppression of the Communist movement in the city of Shanghai. Members of Communist labor unions died by the hundreds in this "White Terror." Some naively welcomed the "Revolutionary Army" of Chiang Kai-shek's Northern Expedition, only to be disarmed and shot on the spot. Kuomintang machine-gun fire raked a peaceful demonstration of workers on April 13, killing three hundred. "Those who resisted," reported one eyewitness, "were either killed on the spot or wounded . . . Many of the wounded were left to die where they dropped. It was an hour before the streets were cleared." Many of the wounded were carried away and buried with the dead.

This brutal suppression in Shanghai was soon followed by the elimination of Communists throughout the country. Chiang Kai-shek was in complete control of the Kuomintang forces. Within a year, his troops had occupied most of China, and the nation was unified under his command.

Chiang Kai-shek was certainly one of the craftiest political leaders of twentieth-century China. His rise to power during the Northern Expedition and his elimination of the Communist Party (except for a small remnant which Mao Tse-tung led into the mountains near his home province of Hunan in south central China), was a masterpiece of political manipulation. Even his marriage in 1927 to the daughter of a leading Shanghai banker had the air of a political alliance about it. He filled key government posts with close friends whose loyalty he could rely upon even if their abilities were questionable. His ability for political intrigue and manipulation enabled him to continue as ruler of all China from 1927 to 1949, when he fled to the island of Taiwan (or Formosa).

Chiang was a lean, nervous, unusually tense man who gave incredible attention to detail. His insistence on over-

seeing every aspect of Chinese life led him to take up scores of official posts ranging from President of China, Chief Executive of the Kuomintang and Commander-in-Chief of the Army, Navy and Air Force, to President of the National Glider Association and President of the National Spiritual Mobilization Council.

Transporting corpses after an anti-Communist massacre by Nationalist forces in Canton in 1928.

Chiang approached the problems of modern China as a conservative moralist. As a Confucianist, he failed to see any basic injustice in the inequality of rich and poor. He believed that if people behaved in a strictly moral fashion, China's social problems would disappear. Chiang's own morality combined Christianity and Confucianism. He had been converted to Christianity when he married the American-educated Madame Chiang, and maintained a strict Puritanical code of ethics. In his personal life, Chiang was distant and reserved. He never smoked or gambled, and he rarely drank. Dancing was frowned upon in Chiang's China. Though he lived in large mansions and was driven about in big black limousines, he believed in frugality and was personally incorruptible.

Even more fundamental than his Christianity was his insistence on the old Confucian virtues of sincerity, righteousness, and above all, loyalty and filial piety. It was this last fact that set Chiang apart from the progressives in modern China. After the May 4th Movement, the old Confucian values had been under constant attack by Chinese intellectuals. The youth and intellectuals perceived that China had fallen into her unhappy state because the government had been in the hands of old men tied to the values of the past. But Chiang did not see things that way. Though, as a nationalist, he was disturbed by China's weakness, he thought the roots of her weakness lay not in her ancient tradition or social inequality, but in the subversion of her moral fiber by the imperialists in the foreign concessions. He wrote:

China's five-thousand-year-old traditions of diligence, thrift and simplicity, of cotton shoes and a simple diet, of women weaving and men farming, were completely undermined by the opium, gambling, prostitutes and thugs of the [foreign] concessions.

As a prescription to save the nation from both Western and Communist "imperialism," Chiang urged a reassertion of China's traditional ethics. What he proposed was a return to the kind of loyalty and filial piety that characterized Confucianism:

To fulfill the principle of complete loyalty to the state and of filial piety toward the nation; to be altruistic and not seek personal advantage; to place the interests of the state above those of family; such is the highest standard of loyalty and filial piety.

And thus, when the intellectuals demanded individual freedom, when critics pointed out the widespread corruption among government officials, when peasants cried for relief from the oppressive rents and taxes of gentry and government, Chiang's solution was always the same—a stricter morality, the old morality of obedience and loyalty to "superiors."

In the end, Chiang Kai-shek, like Yüan Shih-k'ai, was trying to meet the problems of the present by returning to the ways of the past.

5
THE RISE
OF COMMUNISM

The Birth of Peasant Communism and the Kiangsi Soviet

In 1926, just half a year before Chiang Kai-shek unleashed the "White Terror" against his Communist working-class allies in Shanghai, Mao Tse-tung made a journey into the backward countryside of his native province, Hunan. As Mao tells us in the report on his trip, "I saw and heard of many strange things of which I had hereto been unaware. Many of the hows and whys of the peasant movement were the exact opposite of what the gentry in [the big cities of] Hankow and Changsha are saying."

Mao's trip into the Hunan countryside, which he had left as a youth some 15 years before, was a journey back not only to his own beginning, but to the roots of China—the peasants. In several important country areas, Mao found that the peasants had risen up against their landlords in an "upsurge of the peasant movement" which he described as "a colossal event." It surprised even Mao, who as a member of the young Chinese Communist Party had spent most of his time organizing among factory, transportation and mine workers. From Hunan he wrote:

In a very short time, in China's central, southern and north-ern provinces, several hundred million peasants will rise like a mighty storm, like a hurricane, a force so swift and violent that no power, however great, will be able to hold it back. They will smash all the trammels that bind them and rush forward on the road to liberation. They will sweep all the imperialists, warlords, corrupt officials, local strongmen, and evil gentry into their graves. Every revolutionary party and every revolutionary comrade will be put to the test, to be accepted or rejected. It will be their choice. There are three alternatives: To march at their head and lead them? To trail behind them carping and criticizing? Or to stand in their way and oppose them? Every Chinese is free to choose, but events will force you to make the choice quickly.

These were bold but prophetic words for a young man whose party had been ordered by Stalin to organize a Chinese revolution from the cities, only to be completely destroyed several months later by Chiang's executioners, during those fateful days in Shanghai.

By 1927, the repression in the cities had become so great that Mao again took to the hills, to a remote region on the Hunan-Kiangsi border area near where he had been the previous year. But this time Mao went for good. These wild mountains, which came to be known as the Kiangsi Soviet, were covered with bamboo groves and pine forests replete with tigers, deer and pheasant. The valleys produced rice, tea and beans and *t'ung* oil for cooking. Only about five villages with populations as large as 2,000 people existed within the 150 mile circumference of the Soviet. The area was primitive but virtually self-sufficient, and it provided a relatively safe sanctuary.

In this inaccessible region, Mao joined up with Generals Ch'en Yi, Lin Piao and Chu Teh, all destined to play important roles in the Chinese revolution over the next forty-five years. Numbering only about 1,000 men at first, the Red Army grew quickly to over 50,000 men (still with only 4,000 rifles) by 1928.

For his independence and audacity in defying Party headquarters and leaving the cities, Mao was rebuked and dismissed from the Party's Politburo. For the Chinese Communist Party, now underground, was still being directed by the heavy hand of Stalin thousands of miles away in Moscow. Knowing little of the conditions of the peasantry and countryside in China, Stalin had ordered the Party to continue clandestine organization of workers in the cities, in keeping with Marxist theory that revolution must be made by the industrial proletariat of city factory workers.

China's First Peasant Revolutionaries

These were extremely difficult years for Mao and the small Red Army. The most immediate problem was survival. Not only were they constantly harassed and attacked by Chiang's German-trained troops, but there were many internal feuds and disagreements as well. Mao was not yet the unrivaled leader of later years.

Mao and the Kiangsi leadership brought the message of class warfare and revolution to the remote countryside. It caught on easily amidst the dissatisfaction of peasants, who worked long hours on rented land, only to pay a half or more of their harvest to an absentee landlord. There had been many peasant revolts in Chinese history, but never before had they been combined with the notion that justice warranted completely overturning the society, so that the peasant could control his own life, land and community.

The most basic revolutionary idea that was brought to the Kiangsi Soviet was land reform. This meant the confiscation of land from large land-holders, by force if necessary, and the repartition of that land among all the needy local inhabitants. One can understand how a peasant who had never owned his own fields, or had owned only a part of them, would have been justifiably enthusiastic over such a plan, especially when he knew that the Red Army would defend his new title against a landlord returning with Nationalist troops. The Communists were meticulous in explaining to the peasants that Chiang Kai-shek was the defender of the landlords, while they were the defenders of the landless. They took great pains to portray this in class terms, namely, that there were the rich in whose interest the Nationalists ruled, and the poor in whose interest the Communists were striving to establish a government. The message was clear to all who were poor.

As a consequence, a furious and often uncontrolled wave of violent expropriations and executions swept the countryside in the Communist-held areas. Mao himself admits of this period, that the peasants and newly formed Peasant Associations often,

fine the local tyrants and evil gentry, they demand contributions from them, and then smash their sedan chairs. People swarm into the houses of the local tyrants and evil gentry who are against the peasant associations, slaughter their pigs and consume their grain. They even get into the ivory-inlaid beds for a minute or two which belong to the young ladies in the households. At the slightest provocation they make arrests, crown the arrested with tall paper hats and parade them through the villages saying, "You dirty landlords, now you know who we are!" Doing whatever they like and turning everything upside down, they have created a kind of terror in the countryside.

The results of this early land reform were often chaotic and brutal. Mao and others admit to many excesses during this period: landlords were beaten, some middle peasants were unfairly branded as landlords, valuable farm equipment and draft animals were destroyed, crops were neglected. As the years passed, however, this early recklessness was tempered by a realization that greater discipline and control over destruction were necessary to keep food production up. Mao cautioned against alienating the productive "middle peasants," or medium-sized landholders, who might join the peasant associations and bring their knowledge and organizational skills with them. But clearly, in this matter of land reform, the Communists had hit on the problem nearest to the peasants' hearts. And it is understandable how the Red Army was able to recruit a sizable and devout following from among these "liberated" peasants.

It was not long until the new peasant associations, which governed in place of the old gentry, organized their own "standard household militia" or armed force. They began to set up "spear corps" armed with simple double-edged blades mounted on long shafts; there were allegedly 100,000 in one county alone. As Mao describes it, "This multitude equipped with spears . . . is a new born armed power, the mere sight of which makes the local tyrants and evil gentry tremble."

Many mistakes had been made during the chaotic years of the young Kiangsi Soviet (from 1927 to 1934). But much had been learned from these mistakes. Mao and his cohorts had brought the first coherence and organization to the disorganized peasant unrest in the Kiangsi-Hunan border area hills. A government, schools, crude medical facilities and an army had taken root. Slowly the Soviet area had grown, as more and more troops and their commanders defected from the Nationalist armies and more and more peasants joined the Communist ranks. A whole new self-governing world grew up, beyond the effective reach of even Moscow and Stalin, who had never had much faith in the possibility of a peasant revolution. The Kiangsi period was one of experimentation, of the first bold, and often clumsy attempts at peasant democracy. But after all the mistakes were accounted for, what remained was the power of this as yet untried idea. The vision of a *Chinese Communist* society, not simply a Communist society, was being born.

These accomplishments were, indeed, extraordinary when viewed in comparison with the backwardness that prevailed in the rest of rural China, nominally under the control of Chiang and his warlord coalition. They were carried out by an infant Soviet government, at war with the Nationalists and with no aid or support from any outside power. By the end of 1934, when the Red Army was finally forced to break through the armies of Chiang's fifth "extermination campaign," and struggle north to a new home, it was clear to anyone who knew the Communists, that what had transpired in the Kiangsi hills was no marginal or dead end operation. Mao was later reputed to have said, "Whoever wins the peasants will win China. Whoever solves the land question will win the peasant."

In 1928 Mao wrote, "How to deal with the enemy and how to fight have become the central problems of our daily life." The Red Army was a ragtag bunch of men, extremely poorly armed and poorly fed. Almost all their arms and equipment had to be captured in skirmishes with Chiang's Nationalist troops. If a man was lucky, he had a rifle and five rounds of ammunition. Others fought with staffs or sharpened bamboo poles. Medical supplies for even the "heavy casualties" were often non-existent. Few goods of any kind could be gotten back into the mountainous Soviet region through Chiang's blockade Mao wrote:

. . . besides rice, each man gets only five cents a day for cooking oil, salt, firewood, and vegetables, and it is even hard to keep this up . . . Cold as the weather is, many of our men are still wearing two suits of clothes of single thickness. Fortunately we are inured to hardship. Furthermore all share alike in the same hardships: everybody from the army commander down to the cook lives on a daily fare worth five cents, apart from grain . . . Thus the soldiers harbor no resentment against anyone.

Between 1927 and 1934, Chiang Kai-shek launched five massive "bandit extermination" campaigns against the small Red Army. He mobilized over a million men, but the Communist troops learned to fight as a guerrilla army—to indulge in hit and run raids, to attack only when they were strong, and retreat when they were weak. Like mosquitoes, the small mobile units of the Red Army continued to harass Chiang's huge, immobile force. But still Mao was forced to admit that "We have an acute sense of loneliness and are every moment longing for the end of such a lonely life."

The last of the "bandit" extermination campaigns was launched in 1933. So intent was Chiang on succeeding, that he put some 400,000 men in the field, built hundreds of miles of roads, and thousands of small fortifications with interconnecting fields of machine-gun and artillery fire. These endless operations brought massive destruction to the civilian population. An estimated 9,000,000 peasants were killed, while another 1,000,000 starved to death. The price of what Chiang called "pacification" was high. But on October 16, 1934, the Red Army was finally forced to abandon its Kiangsi Soviet and flee north. And so began the legendary Long March to Yenan, the Communists' mountain capital until "liberation."

The Long March

By the fall of 1933, seventy-five divisions of German-trained and equipped troops, under the personal command of Chiang Kai-shek, launched the fifth and final extermination campaign. Chiang's objective was to encircle and strangle the Kiangsi Soviet.

In the back of Chiang's mind was the growing threat to China posed by Japanese militarism. The Japanese had attacked Manchuria in 1931, in the hopes of consolidating a position on the Asian mainland before China could unify. Manchuria, an area one quarter the size of China proper, lay to the north of the Great Wall, beyond effective control of the Nationalist government. Then, in retaliation against the anti-Japanese reaction and boycott in Shanghai, Jap-

THE LONG MARCH

THE LONG MARCH *began in October 1934 when the Communists, their forces surrounded (areas circled above), decided to break out. Fleeing to the west in a main force, (solid line) an auxiliary body (dotted line), and other groups, they withstood innumerable attacks and ended up 6,000 miles away and 12 months later in the north. They eventually established their capital at Yenan.*

anese soldiers attacked and devastated much of that city. Fearing further Japanese aggression, Chiang was anxious to destroy the Communists once and for all, lest he be forced to fight on two fronts at once. During the fifth extermination campaign, he threw everything he had against the Red Army for almost two years.

As the knot grew tighter around the Kiangsi Soviet, vital supplies of salt, clothing and medicine were cut off, and for a while, amidst rumors of victory and Mao's death, Chiang believed he had actually succeeded in trapping the Communists. But, as in 1927, his optimism proved premature. On October 2, 1934, Mao, who had just recovered from malaria and a fever of 105°, met with his comrades in a military council. They decided that there was no choice but to try and break through the encirclement and seek a new sanctuary. On October 16, the Long March began.

Among the 100,000, in the vanguard were thirty-five women, including Mao's pregnant wife. Bands of guerrillas were left behind to act as decoys and to fight rear guard actions which gave the others time to escape. Walking day and night, the marchers succeeded in breaking through the lines of Chiang's surprised troops, and began the incredible trek which took Mao's army some 6,000 miles in the ensuing 370 days. Until they reached Yenan on October 20, 1935, the troops marched with almost no rest and little food.

Picture the Red Army, carrying everything including their weapons, food and government records, marching single file across the vastness of China. Winding rivers and Chiang's pursuing troops forced many detours, and they moved first southwest into the jungles of Yunnan, then west to Tibet, north to the deserts of Kansu and the giant Kun Lun mountain range, and finally to Yenan, in Shensi province. All along the route they were forced to fight. By day their long columns were bombed and strafed. Often marching at night under the cover of darkness, they would cover twenty or thirty miles before daybreak. During other

Mao on the Long March.

periods, they marched around the clock, resting for four hours, then marching for four hours, wearing nothing on their feet but straw sandals.

Ch'en Yi, who until recently was the Foreign Minister, wrote about this year-long ordeal in the wilderness:

> *We are short of grain,*
> *For three months we have tasted no meat;*
> *In the summer we eat wild berries, in winter bamboo;*
> *We scour the mountains hunting wild boar,*
> *And catch snakes in the dark of night.*

Another Red Army soldier recalls the Long March:

> *Sometimes we had to spend the night in the open hills . . .*
> *First it was still possible to find some cabin in an out-of-the-*

way spot. But later on the enemy had burned down all the houses and we had to stay in mushroom pickers' sheds or shelters made out of nothing but paper. When these huts were also destroyed by the enemy, we split bamboo poles and wove them into a cover. As the noise of splitting the bamboo could easily be detected by the enemy, we began instead to use the bark of the fir tree. Later we changed to grass huts since the absence of large pieces of bark on the trees made it easy for the enemy to trace us. But we had to abandon even these afterwards as they were also too large to be overlooked during the search and burn campaigns. Finally, each of us was given an umbrella under which we could sleep beneath big trees on rainy days with our backs against one another.

Again and again the Red Army escaped the pursuing Nationalist forces in a series of heroic maneuvers which have become the source of numerous stories and films in modern China. Although by 1935 they had suffered 45,000 casualties, they had already become a legend of invincibility. By October, Mao and his Red Army finally entered Shensi Province in northern China, just below the Great Wall separating China proper from Mongolia. This was to be the new Communist base area for the next ten years, throughout the war with Japan. In its report titled *The Chinese Communist Movement,* published in 1945, the United States Department of War wrote, "The Red Army [during the Long March] has given a brilliant account of itself."

Even on the Long March, the Red Army was more than an army—it was a social force which attempted to spread its influence through every village it passed. The Communist soldiers taught their ideas of land reform, class struggle, and peasant cooperation wherever they went. And they won the confidence of the peasants by their good conduct as they marched, adhering strictly to a set of clearly established rules which every soldier memorized:

1 *Prompt obedience to orders.*

2 *No confiscation whatever from poor peasantry.*

3 *Prompt and direct delivery to the Government for disposal of all goods confiscated from landlords.*

4 *Replace all doors when you leave a peasant's house. [Doors were used by passing troops as board beds]*

5 *Return and roll up straw matting on which you sleep.*

6 *Be courteous and polite to the people and help them when you can.*

7 *Return all borrowed articles.*

8 *Replace all damaged articles.*

9 *Be honest in all transactions with the peasants.*

10 *Pay for all articles purchased.*

11 *Be sanitary, and especially establish latrines a safe distance from people's houses.*

As a result of their efforts, they received invaluable help from the local inhabitants all along the way. And they also learned. The Long March was like an "involuntary and monumental study tour," helping the future leaders of China to a deeper understanding of their nation and its peasants. And finally, the Long March gave the Communists a sense of strength and rightness of their own cause; they had undergone the impossible and survived. It was a rebaptism of the whole Communist movement in China. Once arrived in Yenan, numerically weaker but infinitely stronger in confidence and moral stature, Mao went about building a new Soviet area.

The New Society of Yenan and the Japanese Invasion

On September 11, 1931, the Japanese attacked Manchuria in the famous Mukden Incident, firing the first shots of

World War II in Asia. On January 28, 1932, the Japanese moved southward and savagely attacked the central Chinese coastal city of Shanghai, causing a kind of devastation with which the Chinese would become increasingly familiar over the next long, hard ten years. A reporter for a Chinese magazine described the results of the Japanese attack:

In the distance clouds of dense smoke obscure the horizon ... After a bend in the road, where buses are smashed and overturned, I enter a small village and the smell of burnt timbers mingles with the other acrid smell of roasting human flesh ... Scattered bits of clothing, some of them bloodstained, are noticed. A gang of coolies mingled with farmers and villagers are at work at odd jobs for their new masters [the Japanese], and over them stand Japanese sentries with naked bayonets held horizontally. Those who lag get poked in the loins which enlivens them like sluggish trained mice poked at through a cage.

Everywhere there is a desolate prospect. Vicious fires eat into what yet remains undamaged. Piles of debris are heaped ten, twenty feet high on the side of a brook which unperturbably ambles under a quaint arched bridge, miraculously unhurt. But it is a stream dark with bits of charred wood, broken household articles, pieces of garments. Here and there a swollen corpse floats slowly, or nestles against the bank as if reluctant to abandon the soil where is was rooted.

In the following years, the Japanese moved steadily into Manchuria, and in 1937 they launched a full-scale attack on Peking and north China, aiming their forces at the heartland of China. These were uncertain, grim years for the Chinese. Nationalist sentiment swept through the nation, as the long-standing Japanese threats to overrun China became reality.

But Chiang Kai-shek ignored this surging nationalism in the early 1930s. "You think that it is important that I have

Grief and destruction wrought by the Japanese bombing of Shanghai in 1932.

kept the Japanese from expanding during these years," he said in 1941. "I tell you that it is more important that I have kept the Communists from spreading. The Japanese are a disease of the skin; the Communists are a disease of the heart. They all say that they want to support me, but secretly they want to overthrow me." Chiang allowed the internal threat to take precedence over the external invader, and it was not long before there were massive street demonstrations throughout Nationalist-controlled China, led by students, intellectuals and workers. They demanded to know why Chinese should be killing Chinese, when the very life of the country was imperiled by Japanese soldiers. In north China, the sense of bitterness and betrayal rose to a crescendo, especially among the students, as the people watched the Japanese march through their land unimpeded. The fact that the Communists had officially declared war on Japan in April, 1932, was compelling to many.

"What can we do?" asked one student in a letter to a leftist periodical. The answer came back from Chiang in Nanking, "First unify from within [kill the Communists], then resist the enemy from without." The door remained open to the Japanese while Chiang stubbornly waged his personal war against the Communists. Throughout the early thirties, long after the Communists had declared war on the Japanese, Chiang stalled. Soon, cries of "Traitors to Japanese imperialism!" were heard during the growing number of demonstrations against the government in Nationalist-held territory. National Salvation Committees grew up throughout China. Chiang's answer was to send secret police to jail the leaders.

Meanwhile, in an open move to gain the growing nationalist support, Mao sent word from Yenan that the Communists would cooperate with all anti-Japanese groups, and would immediately change the name of the Communist Youth Corp to the Resist Japan National Salvation Youth Corp. The Communists announced that it would be open to ". . . all patriotic youth whether or not they believe in communism . . . with the sole stipulation that they are willing to resist Japan and save the country." The mass demonstrations and the clumsy government suppression of the protest were all reminiscent of the May 4th Movement, when students had taken to the streets for the first time in 1919. By 1937, untold numbers of activists had been killed, imprisoned, or forced into hiding. In desperation, one student wrote on his dormitory wall:

For ten years
An impoverished student,
I entered Tsinghua [university]
Failing to foresee
That our beautiful land
Would be ours no more.
How sad, how hateful.

A United Front with the Communists

On December 12, 1936, Chiang Kai-shek was kidnapped while on an inspection tour of some troops that were theoretically loyal to him, and it was this incident that finally led to an agreement to cooperate with the Communists against the Japanese.

The troops Chiang was inspecting were commanded by a young warlord, Chang Hsüeh-liang, who had been driven from his Manchurian homeland by the Japanese. Loyal to Chiang and the Nationalists, he had agreed to regroup his troops in northwest China, where they would serve as a containment force around the Communist areas at Yenan. But by 1936 their patience had run out with Chiang. More concerned with Japanese aggression than with communism, they formed a secret cease-fire agreement with the Communists. Learning that Chang Hsüeh-liang's troops were no longer "exterminating" Communists, Chiang went to Sian to find out what was happening. Here he was kidnapped, and released only after he had agreed to enter into a united front with the Communists against Japan.

The Sian Incident was an extreme embarrassment to Chiang (he allegedly lost his false teeth while trying to escape through a window and up a cliff in his nightshirt in the dead of winter), but it finally succeeded in officially uniting China against Japan. It also made it indelibly clear that the Communists had begun to emerge as more than advocates of radical reform; they were now contenders for national leadership in the struggle of the country against Japan.

Communism in Yenan

Communist policies were quite different in Yenan from what they had been in Kiangsi before the Long March. Survival was still an issue, but now, protected by an uneasy peace with Chiang Kai-shek, it became a question of survival against the Japanese. All internal programs and reforms were geared to this task. Violent class warfare against landlords and gentry was tempered, and all groups and parties were encouraged to form a united action front against Japan. But reform was not forgotten. While it may have been temporarily more moderate, it was better organized and better supported.

From the very beginning of their expansion into north China, the Communists stressed mass organization and unity. As they moved into areas captured from the Japanese or into villages from which the landlords and Kuomintang officials had fled in anticipation of Japanese advances, they sought to mobilize every Chinese peasant and worker— man or woman, young or old, literate or illiterate—for the struggle. Numerous groups were set up throughout north and northwest China: the Farmers' National Salvation Corps, the Women's National Salvation Association, People's Self Defense Corps, the Little Vanguards, etc. The Communists sought to teach every individual to defend himself, and thus to erase the traditional line drawn between soldier and citizen. These groups formed what Mao referred to as the "people's army." The Communists were no less vigilant in developing an educational system, health services, traveling entertainment troops, and political education teams. Everywhere one could hear the phrase "K'ai-hui" ("Get together for a meeting"), as the Communists sought to mobilize the

A student teaching an old man to read, in the battle against illiteracy in the Yenan region during World War II.

people from the bottom up in their anti-Japanese struggle.

As a condition for entering the united front with the Nationalists, the Communists had renounced their policy of land confiscation and redistribution. But this did not prevent them from redistributing land that had been abandoned by landlords who fled to the city to escape the war in the countryside or to work for the Japanese. Nor did it prevent them from reducing all rents by twenty-five percent (more in some areas), or from declaring a three-year moratorium on all debts at a simple 10 percent interest, thus freeing many peasants from the hopeless task of paying off loans from landlords with spiraling interest rates. And it did not prevent the Eighth Route Army (the Communist army in north China) from using cavalry horses to plough the fields of peasants who were too poor to own animals. The Communists attempted to institute a system of equal sharing of all responsibilities among all the people, under the rallying slogan, "He who has strength gives strength, he who has money gives money, and he who has knowledge gives skill in the united front against Japan."

During the late thirties and early forties, the Communists became at once saviors of the Chinese in the "liberated areas" from Japan, and saviors of the vast majority of the peasants from exploitation by their richer overlords. The 1945 Report of the United States War Department, *Chinese Communist Movement,* said of this period,

There is no question that the Chinese Communists have produced the best organized movement that modern China has seen, and have knit the people together in support of the Chinese Communist Party and Army as no other government in modern China has been able to do . . . The Eighth Route Army in North China came soon to be considered the benefactors and saviour of the people not only against the Japanese, but also against the rule of landlords and the former warlords who held supreme sway over North China.

As one American official stationed in Communist-controlled north China said, "the peasant appears not only willing but even enthusiastic about paying taxes because he is doing it for the Army, which is protecting him and his possessions, and for the first time in centuries he feels he is getting something in return for his money or goods. It is not the ideology of Communism, that impresses the people. It is the practical results of Communist leadership."

The Bankruptcy of Nationalist China

All this contrasted sharply with the situation in the Nationalist-held zones, where the government had sustained one ego-shattering defeat after another. Unlike the Communists in the liberated areas which dotted north and central China, the Nationalist government did not reach down to the people in the countryside to bolster its war effort. Instead, Chiang turned to the bankers, the landlords, the quasi-warlord army commanders, the United States, and above all, to Germany from which he received more aid and advisors than from any other country, including the U.S., through 1939. Slowly the government and the army became like a head severed from the body of China.

By 1941, the differences between the Communists and the Nationalists, and between Mao and Chiang, were becoming increasingly clear. The war with Japan had put both contenders on trial in the most difficult of circumstances. China was being destroyed by war and her people were perishing by the tens of millions. In the mind of the average Chinese, the struggle was not so much between conflicting ideologies as over the very practical question of which party or which man could hold China together and organize the people to provide for themselves while fighting the Japanese.

By 1941, the united front had become no more than a fiction. Chiang remained fixated on "bandit suppression" (one of his many euphemisms for destroying the Communists), regardless of the popularity of the Communist social programs and the importance of their war effort.

Nationalist armies had almost completely given up the struggle against Japan when, on December 7, 1941, the Japanese attacked Pearl Harbor. Chiang and his commanders breathed a sigh of relief, for at last the United States was in the Pacific war. Victory against Japan would now be only a matter of time, regardless of what Chiang's troops did, so the Nationalists kept their powder dry on the Japanese front, preferring to save it for the day that they would once again move against the Communist "bandits." Then, shortly after Pearl Harbor, in mid-January, 1942, Chiang ordered a secret attack on the Communist Fourth Route Army in central China.

The Fourth Route Army had been reorganized after the formation of the united front in 1938, from elements of the Red Army which had been left behind in Kiangsi at the time of the Long March. Their orders were to remain behind and

conduct diversionary maneuvers and rear guard actions. It was Chiang himself, late in 1937, who had ordered the army reformed, and had assigned it to the Yangtze River Valley in central China, under the command of the able Communist general, Yeh T'ing (who had defected from the Kuomintang in 1927).

Red soldiers helping with the harvest in Yenan.

By 1941, Chiang had begun to be wary of the tremendous success and popularity of the Fourth Route Army. The Communists had coupled their struggle against the Japanese with a whole new economic and political program for the people in the area under their control. Nowhere had the people been more abused by landlords, loan sharks and oppressive gentry than in central China. And in no area had the Nationalists been in more complete control.

The crime for which the Fourth Route Army was attacked, was that they had placed themselves as much against the landlords, and thus against the Kuomintang government, as against the Japanese. As a result, thousands of people swelled their ranks, and the strength of the Fourth Route Army grew from 12,000 in 1938 to over 125,000 regulars in 1941, backed up by some 500,000 organized local militia. All this was taking place during a time when the Nationalists were forced to lasso throngs of young men coming out of movie theaters to keep recruitment in their own armies up to partial strength.

After vain protest against Chiang's order to move, the Fourth Route Army began to evacuate, but as a column of some 12,000 soldiers, teachers, students, nurses, hospital orderlies and wounded made their way to the Yangtze River, they were suddenly ambushed and slaughtered by the Nationalists. Two thousand were killed and four thousand were wounded. The Nationalists denied all knowledge of the incident, and tried to suppress all news dispatches reporting its occurrence to the United States.

Nationalist-Communist relations never recovered from this betrayal. Chiang had once again made the mistake of trying to exterminate the Communists by sudden violence. Once again he had missed the point—that there was an idea and a social movement at the roots of the Communist armies, which accounted for their dedication. T. V. Soong, Chiang's own brother-in-law and cabinet member, confided to Edgar Snow, "Chiang simply does not think people count. His worst weakness is that he relies on military force alone." Chiang counted his guns and his money, while Mao counted his recruits.

From the Fourth Route Army incident in 1941, until the Japanese surrender in 1945, the Nationalist armies did little to fight the Japanese and much to rid China of Communists. American attempts to supply and train Chiang's armies were welcomed, in fact demanded. But when criticism was leveled at military performance or the operation of his government, Chiang would peevishly threaten to drop out of the war completely and sign a separate peace with the Japanese. This put American military men in a difficult position, at a time when the Japanese seemed perilously close to success in the Pacific.

Some Americans, like General Joseph Stilwell, Commander-in-Chief of the China-India-Burma theater, recognized the Communists as the only effective, ready fighting force in China. Discouraged by what he had seen in the Nationalist capital, Chungking, and by his experience with the Nationalist commanders, he proposed that the United States give aid to the Communists in their struggle against the Japanese in north China. Chiang, of course, adamantly refused to accept such a plan, since he viewed the Communists as more of a threat than the Japanese. Stilwell wrote:

Chiang Kai-shek is confronted with an idea, and that defeats him. He is bewildered by the spread of Communist influence. He can't see that the mass of Chinese people welcome the Reds as being the only visible hope of relief from crushing taxation, the abuse of the Army and the terror of Tai Li's Gestapo [the Nationalists' secret police]. Under Chiang Kai-shek they now begin to see what they may expect: greed, corruption, favoritism, more taxes, a ruined currency, terrible waste of life, callous disregard of all the rights of men.

No more graphic description of the difference between the Nationalist camp and the Communist camp exists than in eye witness accounts of the two capitals. A *Time* magazine correspondent, Theodore White, described Chungking:

The slime in the streets was inches thick [in the winter], and people carried the slippery mud as they went from bedroom to council chamber and back. There was no escaping the chilly moisture except by visiting the handful of people who lived in modern homes in which coal was burned. The crowded huddled refugee population, cramped together in their jerry built shacks, could only warm their fingers over expensive charcoal pots or go to bed early. Everyone shivered until the summer came; then the heat settled down, and the sun glared. Dust coated the city almost as thickly as mud during the winter time. Moisture remained in the air, perspiration dripped and prickly heat ravaged the skin . . . Swarms of bugs emerged . . . Meat spoiled; there was never enough water for washing, dysentery spread and could not be evaded . . . Sewage piled up in the gutters and smelled; mosquitoes bred in stagnant pools of water deep in the ruins and malaria flourished.

And all the while, the failing Nationalist government was held together as much by the Japanese bombing of Chungking as anything else.

A U.S. Army Colonel, head of the United States Observer Mission at the Communist capital, Yenan, described how strange a contrast it was to come there from Chungking, which had been overrun with secret police and the symbols of a government cut off from the people:

One reason a good many people, including myself, had generally a favorable impression of the Communist regime in Yenan was that the overall look of things was one which most Americans were inclined to regard with favor. In Chungking we were accustomed to seeing police and sentries everywhere. In Yenan there was not even a sentry as far as I could see, posted at Headquarters 18th Group Army [the Observer Mission]. If there was anyone on guard at Mao-Tse-tung's unpretentious place of residence, he was not in evidence to the casual passerby.

When Chairman Mao appeared in public, as he frequently did, he traveled on foot, or in the one battered truck, with enclosed cab, which as far as I ever knew, constituted the Communists' sole motor transport. There was no parade of long black cars, often moving at high speed, which one saw

in Chungking when the Generalissimo traversed the streets, and no cordons of guards and secret service operative such as always surrounded him in public.

Mao's cave in Yenan, now a museum.

The Communist War Effort and Political Program

But perhaps the most telling fact of all was that even the Japanese viewed the Communists as the greatest military and political threat to their efforts to conquer China. Japanese war communiques made frequent mention of battles with "bandits," "mopping up operations" and "pacification campaigns" in north China. In 1943, General Hata, Commander-in-Chief of the Japanese Expeditionary Forces in China, spoke in a press interview of the Communist troops as ". . . the chief disturbing factors endangering peace and order," (under the Japanese puppet government). The Communists continued attacking the Japanese with the kind of guerrilla warfare they had learned in Kiangsi against Chiang's troops. They seldom were able, or even tried, to defeat major Japanese units, but they did succeed in harassing the Japanese and preventing them from stabilizing or administrating the areas that they had occupied. In their own areas, the Communists developed excellent "people's" intelligence networks, through close cooperation with the local militia organizations and village mobilization committees. A few Communist guerrillas could tie up a whole army by raiding key communications centers and attacking poorly defended supply columns. The Japanese were reduced to waging costly, massive operations, like a fumbling giant playing hide-and-go-seek with midgets. But unfortunately, they released their frustration on the people in their "three-all policy"—kill all, burn all, loot all. The result of this scorched earth policy was simply to drive the people further into the arms of the Communists, who provided their only defense and their only aid in rebuilding damaged fields, homes and lives.

The Communists effectively used the war and the Japanese threat to spread both their influence and their control throughout north China. This greatly disturbed the Nationalists, but they seemed totally incapable of competing with their adversary for the loyalty of the common man.

In 1944, a U.S. Foreign Service officer who had been stationed with the Communists in Yenan wrote, "The Chinese Communists have become the most dynamic force in China and are challenging the Kuomintang for control of the country." Two months later, he went on to describe the state of total mobilization in the north Chinese countryside as leading to "complete solidarity of Army and people."

At the root of Mao's success was a convincing vision of what a "New China" would look like. His vision was of a nation and a society in which the class distinctions between rich and poor, gentry and peasantry, and even men and women, would be destroyed. Realistically, Mao could see

that there would be little chance of reform in China without some violence, for unless the poor became powerful, they would be ignored. And when and if they became powerful enough or troublesome enough, they would be met with defensive violence by the privileged few. Mao had studied Marxist theories of class warfare well, and he knew that there could be no such thing as "peaceful revolution" in China, where the ruling class had always maintained itself in power by violence. But Mao was also a realist, and everyone who was willing to resist the Japanese was welcomed during these war years, in what Mao called "New Democracy."

"New Democracy" in Yenan reflected this realism. It was a coalition of almost all classes and groups in China who wished to fight the Japanese. Every citizen participated politically on the local level to elect representatives to village committees and People's Congresses. A basic unity was as-

Madame Sun Yat Sen's revolutionary school in Yenan.

sured among the diverse groups by the threat of invasion.

"New Democracy" did not mean, however, that anyone could say anything. Freedom was denied to traitors and Japanese spies. There were definite limits to freedom of expression, for instance, if it appeared to threaten the war effort. But generally speaking, there was a tolerance which reflected the broad spectrum of people who made up the Communist coalition.

Many observers during the early forties were fooled into thinking that Chinese Communism had changed its nature. Many thought "New Democracy" was the final goal of the Communists, and that Mao was just a moderate "agrarian reformer." Had they read Mao's writings, they would certainly have seen their error, for Mao was very clear about his intentions. "We are always revolutionaries," he said, "and we are never reformists." He went on to explain how "New Democracy" was destined to end just as it had begun, and the next stage of the revolution, socialism, would follow. He made no secret of the fact that he believed "acts of violence" would reoccur as one class struggled to overthrow the other, first in the Chinese countryside and finally in the cities.

Famine and the Land Problem

By the end of the war, China was in a state of total collapse. Famine had swept the country, brutalizing the people even more than the war. Communist-held areas had steadily expanded across north and northwest China, particularly after V-J Day, when the Communists took control over many areas from the surrendering Japanese. In these sections of China, land reform, the absence of corruption and good administration alleviated much human suffering.

But in the Nationalist-held areas—the big cities, land adjacent to major roads, railways and other communication lines in north China, and most of central China—the situation was often critical. Theodore White, the *Time* reporter, described the Honan famine in Nationalist-held territory in 1944, and the people fleeing starvation:

Old women hobbled along on bound feet, stumbled and fell; no one picked them up. Other old women rode pickaback on the strong shoulders of their sons, staring through coal black eyes at the hostile sky. Young men, walking alone strode at a quicker pace with all their possessions in a kerchief over their shoulder. Small mounds of rags by the roadside marked where the weak had collapsed; sometimes a few members of the family stared at the body in silent perplexity. The children leaned on their staffs like old men; some carried bundles as large as themselves; others were dream walkers whose unseeing eyes were a thousand years old with suffering. Behind them all, from the land of famine a cold wind blew, sending the dust chasing them over the yellow plain . . . There were corpses on the road. A girl no more than seventeen, slim and pretty lay on the damp earth, her lips blue with death; her eyes were open, and the rain fell

Trucks distributing rice from a government store were often followed by hungry people, who collected spillings with pans and brushes.

on them. People chipped at bark, pounded it by the roadside for food; vendors sold leaves at a dollar a bundle. A dog digging at a mound was exposing a human body. Ghostlike men were skimming the stagnant pools to eat the green slime of the waters.

White goes on to describe the government's reaction, and how they appropriated valueless inflated paper money, instead of grain, as relief for their dying citizens.

Stupidity and inefficiency marked the relief effort. But the grisly tragedy was compounded even further by the actions of the constituted local authorities. The peasants, as we saw them, were dying. They were dying by the roads, in the mountains, by the railway stations, in their mud huts, in their fields. As they died the Government continued to wring from them the last possible ounce of tax. The money tax the peasant had to pay on his land was a trivial matter; the basic tax exacted from him was the food tax, a basic percentage of all the grain that he raised, and despite the fine-sounding resolution of remittance in Chungking, the tax was being extorted from him by every device the army and the provincial authorities could dream up. The Government, in county after county, was demanding more actual poundage of grain than he had raised on his acres. No excuses were allowed; peasants who were eating elm bark and dried leaves had to haul their last sack of seed grain to the tax collector's office. Peasants who were so weak they could barely walk had to collect fodder for the army's horses, fodder that was more nourishing than the filth they were cramming into their mouths. Peasants who could not pay were forced to the wall. They sold their cattle, their furniture, and even their land to buy grain to meet the tax quotas.

Former Minister of Finance, T. V. Soong, after his appointment in 1948 to the governorship of Kwangtung Province,

said, "We are not planning a land reform in Kwangtung because the system we have had here for years is satisfactory." Soong did not mean to be facetious.

It was not long before peasants, driven by desperation and pent up hostility, turned on the landlords, and the government and army which defended them. With blind rage they attacked their tormentors, pillaged their granaries, burned their walled houses and often killed the occupants. After the Japanese surrender in 1945, peasant uprisings swept north China. In a sense, "New Democracy" ended in rural China as class turned on class. Often clashes were provoked when landlords who had fled to the cities during the war, returned with Nationalist troops to demand their land back from the peasants to whom it had been distributed by the Communists. Sometimes hunger led to outbreaks. Other times peasants mobilized to "settle old scores," as they said. Young Communist cadres, or trained Party organizers, flocked to the countryside to goad the peasants into recognizing their dismal plight and encourage them to dare to act. But they seemed to have little control over what finally developed into a spontaneous and bloody campaign of land confiscation. One American reporter in China at

As the value of paper money sank, the Kuomintang decided to distribute 40 grams of gold per person. In December 1948, a "gold rush" resulted with thousands coming out to wait in line for their gold.

the time described the passion that engulfed the countryside as a mass of ". . . radiant hopes and murderous hates that the Chinese peasant poured into the sphere of war and revolution releas[ing] a flood of emotional energy that exploded with the force of an atomic bomb within Chinese society, nearly dissolving it."

But the problem was a much deeper one than simply killing all the landlords and redistributing the fields. Two thousand years of psychological subservience had to be destroyed first. The peasant had to learn that he was worth something, that he had strength, that in the new society he would not be consigned to a position of acceptable inferiority as he had been in the days of the old Confucian hierarchy. Frequently the act of confronting his former landlord and master, who had exercised the power of life and death over him and his family, and perhaps beating or killing him, gave to the peasant this new sense of his own efficacy.

An American who watched the process of land reform in a small village in Shansi province wrote,

The ruthless way in which the slightest defiance on the part of the tenants and laborers was suppressed over the years, created in the peasant a deep, almost instinctive, reluctance to mount an attack against the power of the gentry. Revolt after revolt had been crushed during the 20 centuries of gentry rule. Those who raised their heads to lead them had either been bought off or had their heads severed. Their followers had been cut to pieces, burned, flayed, or buried alive. Gentry in the Taihang proudly showed foreign visitors leather articles made from human skin. Such events and such mementos were a part of the cultural heritage of every peasant in China.

It was not easy for a simple peasant to think in terms of "changing heaven." He had many fears. The situation of the peasant had never been changed—how could it be changed

now? Would he be punished? Would the Red Army really
come and support him, or would the Nationalists return and
execute all the rebels? These were questions for which the
peasant had no certain answer. But once he had freed his
mind and gained new confidence, the poor peasant was like an
uncontrollable tornado. Below is a description of what hap-
pened in one village:

*That same day a mass meeting was called in a great square
field south of the town, not far from the river. About eighty
people came to complain against Wang the landlord, while
the rest of the village watched—among them Wang's wife
and daughter.*

*In the course of the morning and afternoon, the crowd ac-
cused the landlord of many crimes, including betrayal of
Resistance members to the Japanese, robbing them of grain,
forcing them into labor gangs. At last, he was asked if he
admitted to the accusations.*

*"All these things I have done," he said, "but really it was not
myself who did it, but the Japanese."*

*He could not have chosen worse words. Over the fields now
sounded an angry roar, as of the sea, and the crowd broke
into a wild fury. Everybody shouted at once, proclaiming
against the landlord's words. Even the nonparticipating by-
standers warmed to something akin to anger.*

*Then above the tumult of the crowd came a voice louder
than the rest, shouting: "Hang him up!"*

*The chairman of the meeting and the cadres were disre-
garded. For all that the crowd noticed they did not exist.*

*The crowd boiled around Wang and somewhere a rope went
swishing over a tree. Willing hands slung one end of the
rope around Wang's waist. Other eager hands gave the rope
a jerk. Wang rose suddenly and came to a halt in mid-air
about three feet above the earth. And there he hung, his
head down, his stomach horizontal and his legs stretched*

out—a perfect illustration of what the Chinese call a "duck's swimming form."

About his floating body, the crowd foamed, anger wrinkling their foreheads and curses filling their mouths. Some bent down and spit in the landlord's eyes and others howled into his ears.

As he rose from the ground, the landlord felt a terror which mounted higher as his position became more uncomfortable. Finally, he could bear it no longer and shouted: "Put me down. I know my wrongs. I admit everything."

The spite of the crowd, however, was not so easily assuaged and they only answered the landlord's pleas with shouts: "Pull him up! He's too low! Higher! Higher!"

After a while the anger of the people abated and cooler heads counseled, "If we let him die now, we won't be able to settle accounts with him." Then they allowed him to come down for a rest.

At this point, the wife of Original Fortune Lee came up close to Wang and said in a plaintive voice: "Somebody killed my husband. Was it you?"

Wang's face which had grown red from hanging in the air slowly was drained of all color. "No, I did not do it," he said.

"Tell the truth," said the crowd. "You can admit everything to us and nothing will happen. But if you don't tell us the truth, we will hang you up again."

"No, it was not me."

These words were hardly out of his mouth before someone jerked on the rope and the landlord flew into the air again. This time the crowd let him hang for a long while. Unable to bear the pain, Wang finally said: "Let me down. I'll speak."

Then, between sobs and sighs, he told how he and his son

had seized Original Fortune Lee as he was walking home from the meeting, tied his hands together, held his head under water until he was dead and then had thrown him in the river, thinking he would float away.

A cry of rage went up as Wang finished speaking.

"You've already killed three of our men in the war," said Liu Kwang. "That could be excused. But now your own life can never repay us for the crimes you've done."

Again Wang was hung up and this time many shouted: "Let him hang until he is dead." But others said: "That is too quick; he must first have a taste of the suffering we've had."

At dusk, they let Wang down once more and put him in a cave under guard again.

As soon as the meeting was over, twenty or thirty men went to the landlord's house, drove the wife and daughter out of doors and sealed the house. The two women went to a nearby village to stay with relatives.

That evening the five cadres and those who had taken an active part in the struggle against the landlord walked around the village to listen to the gossip and sample public opinion. Such words were heard as: "Serves him right; he's so wicked. This is too light for him. Just count his sins."

Later that night another meeting of those of the village who wanted to struggle against the landlord was held in a court-yard. This time a hundred and twenty people attended.

When the cadres asked: "How do you feel? Have you done well?" the answer came back: "Oh fine! Fine!"

But exactly what to do with the landlord was a problem for which the people at first had no solution. Half of those in the meeting thought he should be beaten to death. A few said: "He is too old." Some had no ideas at all. Others thought that his clerk, the rich farmer Shih Tseng-hua, should be bound up with him at the same time in the *struggle. This suggestion, however, was voted down when someone pointed out: "You should always collect the big melons in the fields first. So we should cut off the big head first."*

It was decided that Wang must die for his murders. But how? Should he be sent to the district government to be punished, or should the people kill him or what?

"If he is tried before a court-martial for treason," said a farmer, "then there will be only one bullet, and that is too cheap for Wang. We ought to kill him first and report to the government afterward."

"Who dares kill him?" asked a farmer doubtfully.

At this everyone shouted at once: "We dare. We dare. He bayoneted our militiamen to death and we can also do that to him."

Three days after this meeting, the whole village breakfasted early, and shortly after sunrise, seven hundred men and women, including visitors from neighboring villages, many armed with pig knives, hoes, sickles, swords, and spears went out to the large field south of town where the landlord was to be killed. The cadres had written down Wang's crimes on large pieces of paper and these, hanging by ropes from the trees, now fluttered in the breeze.

"Traitor Wang Chang-ying killed three militiamen and one active farmer of the village," one said.

"Sinful Landlord Wang grafted money and grain during the War of Resistance," said another.

"Wang Chang-ying shifted the tax burden onto the people and looted the village," said a third.

A shout went up from the crowd as Landlord Wang was led onto the field. Three guards marched him, pale and shaking, to a willow tree where he was bound up. With his back

广大翻身。贫苦群众怒火地站起来，在政治上树立起自己的优势，打倒万恶的地主阶级。这是青海省土改百苦农民向恶霸地主进行坚决斗争的干事。

against the tree, the landlord looked once at the crowd but quickly bent his head toward the ground again.

A slight shiver of apprehension went through the audience. They could not believe their enemy was helpless here before them. He was the lamb led to slaughter, but they could not quite believe they were going to kill him.

Ma Chiu-tze stepped before the crowd and called for attention. "Now the time has come for our revenge," he announced in a trembling voice. "In what way shall we take revenge on this sinful landlord? We shall kill him."

As he said this, he turned around and slapped Wang sharply across the face.

The crack of palm against cheek rang like a pistol shot on the morning air. A low animal moan broke from the crowd and it leaped into action.

A people's court during land reform; a peasant accuses a big landlord.

The landlord looked up as he heard the crowd rushing on him. Those nearest saw his lips move and heard him say: "Two words, two words please."

The man closest shouted: "Don't let him speak!" and in the same breath swung his hoe, tearing the clothes from the bound man's chest and ripping open the lower portion of his body.

The landlord gave one chilling shriek and then bowed his head in resignation. The crowd was on him like beasts. Their faces had turned yellow and their eyes rolled. A big farmer swung his pig knife and plunged it directly into the landlord's heart. His body quivered—even the tree shook— then slumped, but still the farmer drew his knife in and out, again and again and yet once again.

Landlord Wang was quickly dead, but the rage of the crowd would not abate.

The field rang with the shouts of maddened people.

"It is not enough to kill him."

"We must put him in the open air."

"We must not allow him to be buried for three days."

But such convulsive passions do not last long. They burn themselves out. Slowly, the anger of the crowd cooled. The body of the landlord might rot in the open air and it was better that his wife and daughter be allowed to get him.

That evening, as the sun was going down behind the mountain, the landlord's wife and daughter brought a mule cart slowly across the field to where their husband and father lay. They wept no tears, but silently lifted the mutilated body into the cart and drove away.

Few saw them come and few saw them go. And no one said a word. For there was nothing left to say. The struggle against the landlord was ended.

Stone Wall Village had turned over.

Civil War

As usual, the Communists coupled their social revolution
after 1945 with military action. While land reform was
sweeping inland China, the Red Army waged war against
the Nationalists. All attempts at negotiations, mostly ar-
ranged by Americans, came to nought. A coalition government of Communists and Nationalists was not workable.

Japan's surrender in August, 1945 set off a monumental
race between the Nationalists and the Communists to take
over the once-occupied territory. All over China, clashes
broke out. Chiang raced his armies in several directions at
once—to the coast, to north China, and to Manchuria, occupied by the Russians, according to the Yalta agreement.
Chiang was determined to conquer rather than compromise.
He insisted to the world that he was the only Chinese leader
and that the Nationalist government was the only legitimate
government, but his stubbornness did nothing to explain away
the vast areas under Communist control and administration,
nor did it take into account the fact that the Red Army was
growing daily with new recruits and defectors from
Chiang's own ranks.

Theoretically Chiang was right—he was Generalissimo
Chiang, leader of the Republic of China. But in realistic
terms he was one of two leaders, and China was a divided
nation. Like ice in hot sun, his strength was melting with
each passing day, but this fact he refused to recognize. Not
only had he badly overextended his forces all across China,
controlling no more than the cities, and leaving the countryside to the Communists, but he had made the costly mistake
of sending southerners to the north, and central Chinese to
the northwest, where dialects were different and customs
new. The soldiers were alienated from the local inhabitants
and unwelcomed by them. Chiang's army was not a "people's
army."

By 1947, it was clear that the Communists, who had
shown a surprising willingness to at least temporary com-

promise with the Nationalists after the Japanese defeat, now rejected such a solution. In the intervening years they had further consolidated their positions and strengthened their armies, and Chiang's position had markedly deteriorated.

General Albert Wedemeyer, commander of American troops in the China theater and Chief-of-Staff to Chiang Kai-shek, described the hopeless situation as he saw it in 1947:

In Manchuria, I was told by many sources that the Central Government armies [Nationalists] were welcomed enthusiastically by the people as deliverers from Japanese oppression. Today, after several months of experience with the Central Government armies, the people experience a feeling of hatred and distrust because the officers and enlisted men were arrogant and rude. Also they stole and looted freely; their general attitude was that of conquerors rather than deliverers.

While the Red Army was urging land reform, Chiang's armies (often underpaid because greedy commanders embezzled the money), were looting, pillaging and bringing misery to the inhabitants. By the end of the Civil War in 1949, whole divisions of Chiang's troops had defected or surrendered to the Communists. In response to popular pleas and endless demonstrations calling for an end to the Civil War, Chiang sent his secret police and troops to fire on the marchers and arrest their leaders. General Wedemeyer reported:

Secret Police operate widely, very much as they do in Russia and as they did in Germany. People disappear. Students are thrown into jail. No trials and no sentences. Actions of this nature do not win support for the government. Quite the contrary. Everyone lives with a feeling of fear and loses confidence in the government.

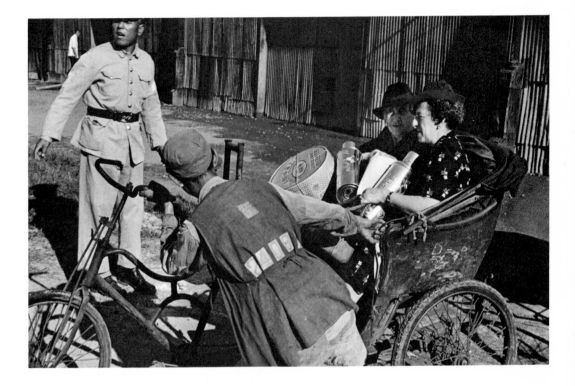

Gradually, the Kuomintang was being taken over by its extreme right wing, composed of people like the reactionary Ch'en Brothers' Clique. Their answer to the Communist threat was simple but stupid—kill them. China's liberals and third party members were ignored, except in so far as they were willing to lend a semblance of democracy to the totalitarian Nationalists. Those who were not imprisoned went into exile, or learned to keep quiet. But many more joined the Communists. By 1947 there were riots throughout Nationalist-held cities, all demanding peace and economic stability. By 1948, the cost of living index was 150,000 times what it had been ten years earlier. Inflation, in spite of American stabilization loans, spiraled out of control. The common man had to pay ten thousand times as much for rice as he had in 1945. A man buying an average-priced pair of shoes could not carry a bundle of money large enough to pay for them. But Chiang insisted that he had things under control and that he would be able to destroy the enemy in a

Europeans preparing to flee China during the waning days of Chiang Kai-shek's regime.

matter of months. To him, the "Communist bandits" were just more soldiers, like his own. And in his own ranks (according to almost every impartial military observer), there was a growing uwillingness to fight in what had become an endless war of Chinese against Chinese. On June 18, 1947, the United States Ambassador to China, John Leighton Stuart, a close friend of Chiang's, reported,

The growing discontent with, or even hostility toward, the government has been stimulated among the intellectuals by the extremely harsh measures against the students, and among the unthinking masses by the mounting costs of livelihood. In simplest terms the complaints center around freedom and food . . . actually much of the strength of the Chinese Communism is due chiefly to the inefficiency and corruption of the Kuomintang and—with an alarming acceleration—to popular loss of faith in the Government.

It is difficult to determine at just what point in history a government loses its right to represent its people, and becomes more of a burden on those people than a help. But by 1948 that point had clearly come and passed for Chiang Kaishek and his government.

Every month brought a new defeat and a loss of territory. Retreat became inevitable, and Chiang was not caught short. Ever since the end of the war he had begun to prepare for a possible move to Taiwan, an island about 400 miles long off the coast of south China. In 1946 and 1947 his generals had ruthlessly suppressed popular independence movements on Taiwan in order to re-establish Nationalist control after the departure of the Japanese. As the mainland ship began to sink, the rat race to Taiwan began. Endless tales abounded of corrupt Kuomintang officials commandeering aircraft and ships to take along everything from their families and money to their cars. While the wealthy were eager to flee, realizing that their kind of life would have little future under Communism, common soldiers had to be ordered at gunpoint to board ships for Taiwan. Most left their homes and families behind, and have not seen or heard from them in the intervening twenty-odd years. By the end of 1949, the evacuation was complete, and Chiang weakly proclaimed Taipei the temporary capital of the Republic of China.

The Role of the United States in the Civil War

The United States played an ambiguous role during the Civil War period from 1945–1949, and to this day people disagree violently over what American policy was, and what it should have been. After 1949, cries that we "sold Chiang down the river to the Communists," that "we lost China," all helped obscure the inescapable fact that nothing the U.S.

Students volunteering to fight in Korea.

could have done would have saved a regime so disliked and inept as Chiang's.

Despite its proclaimed neutrality, the United States was deeply involved in the Chinese Civil War from the outset. In the winter of 1945, General George Marshall was sent to China by President Truman to try to effect some sort of coalition government. He had a difficult task trying to skate between the demands and sensitivities of Chiang and the Communist negotiator, Chou En-lai, and ultimately his mission failed. In principle, all U.S. military aid to the Nationalists (we had never given any to the Communists), was to be withheld pending a settlement. However, we did send U.S. marines to north China, and we did agree to provide an airlift for Chiang to fly his troops into Manchuria and north China to prevent the Japanese from surrendering to the Communist Eighth Route Army. We did turn over considerable surplus supplies from the Philippines to Chiang, and as an old war-time ally the United States did diplomatically recognize the Nationalist government. All this made the Communists feel very apprehensive about American neutrality.

Marshall went home in 1947 an exhausted, discouraged man. His inability to make Chiang come to terms with the Communists or reform the Nationalist government had made the Communists distrustful and suspicious of the United States. A mere two years before, Mao had seemed quite hopeful that he could cooperate with the United States in post-war years. In 1945 he had even cabled President Roosevelt, expressing a willingness to come to Washington for political talks, and in 1944–1945 he frequently expressed interest in receiving American assistance to U.S. observers in Yenan. Interviews with him during these years showed a surprising fund of good feelings toward the United States and real optimism for future relations.

But by 1947, all this had changed. Mao was angered at American military support for Chiang, and rightfully distrustful of American anti-Communist forces in Washington, who blindly and without understanding what was happening in China, had finally committed our government to supporting the Nationalists during the desperate years of the Civil War. Had we not interfered, or had our fear of change been less, the whole agony of the Civil War would probably have been considerably more moderate. Even the Russians had played a detached, hands-off game in China during these years. As late as 1945, they again signed a treaty of friendship with Chiang, and dutifully kept an ambassador at the Nationalist capital right up until the bitter end in 1949.

Mao and the Communists won China on their own. Their best ally was the Chinese peasant and the incompetence of Chiang's government. The Mandate of Heaven passed on, and would have passed on regardless of what any outsider could have done. It was the culmination of forty years of readjustment and change that had a logic and dynamic of its own. When Mao marched triumphant into Peking in 1949, with one of the most impressive displays of American military equipment (all captured or bought from the Nationalists) ever seen in Asia, an era died. China had changed out of necessity, to make way for what would prove to be one of the greatest social experiments in history.

6
THE NEW CHINA

Mao Takes Power

In February, 1949, Mao's Liberation Army paraded into an expectant Peking. An American scholar studying there at the time wrote:

As probably the greatest demonstration of Chinese military might in history, the spectacle was enormously impressive . . . The enthusiasm of most [participants] was too obvious to have been feigned, and this notwithstanding that many had been exposed to wind and dust for some four hours before I saw them. I have no doubt that not a few on this day felt a keen sense of personal participation in an event symbolizing the beginning of a new era in Chinese history.

Eight months later, Mao Tse-tung stood before a massive crowd in the ancient capital and proclaimed the birth of the Chinese People's Republic of China. After twenty-two years of revolutionary struggle, resistance to Japan and civil war, Mao and the Chinese Communist Party had emerged as the rulers of the Chinese people. Mao assured his people that, "Our nation will never again be an insulted nation. We have stood up." But he also reminded them that "our revolutionary work is not yet concluded." Behind the Communists stood a wealth of experience in organizing the masses of the Chinese peasantry. But before them lay a China whose society was in chaos and whose economy had been ravaged by decades of war.

The problems which Mao and the Chinese people faced in 1949 were enormous. The country had been at war for almost twenty years—since the Japanese invaded Manchuria and Shanghai in 1931—and much of China's modern industry lay in ruins. The railroads were a shambles. Trade had stopped. Inflation ran wild—prices had increased 85,000 fold in the last six months of the Nationalist regime. Then, before the People's Republic was even one year old, the Korean War began, and American soldiers counterattacked across the border between North and South Korea and marched toward the Chinese frontier. Knowing the intense anti-Communism of the United States, the Chinese feared that the attack was directed ultimately at them.

Through the Indian ambassador in Peking, they made repeated attempts to clarify the situation and to inform the United States and the world how serious they felt the situation to be. But General MacArthur, commander of the United Nations forces in Korea, continued to push north toward the Chinese border. On June 25, 1950, Chinese troops crossed the Yalu River from Manchuria and entered the war.

Immediately, the United States placed an embargo on all trade with China, and the new regime found itself isolated from most of the world. She faced her problems alone, aided only by a certain amount of technical assistance and loans from the Soviet Union—and even that was abruptly cut off in 1960.

With these new difficulties added to the host of barriers to change and progress which had grown up in China over the centuries, we get some sense of the enormity of the task with which Mao Tse-tung was faced. To create a new China out of the ruins of the old, a total revolution of the society was necessary—a revolution which would tackle the contradictions between rich and poor, city and countryside,

intellectuals and manual laborers, industry and agriculture, the elite and the masses. The last twenty years have been the story of that revolution.

A peasant family at dinner in Modern China.

Land Reform

In the two decades before the final Communist victory in 1949, many peasants had joined in the Chinese revolution and carried out land reform in their villages. In the process, peasants were transformed from passive victims of landlord rule to active participants in changing the countryside. But the revolution in the villages did not end with land reform. Land reform only gave equal amounts of land, farm animals and equipment to each peasant. It did not eliminate private ownership of the land or totally solve China's food problem. Each peasant still tilled his own land with his own tools. Inequalities were still possible if one family had better land, or better tools, or a strong ox to pull his plow. But from 1952–1958 the villages of China underwent a long series of transformations. All land, except small private plots which individual families retained for their own use, was turned over to large communes collectively owned by 2,000 families. Work animals and tools were also pooled. Whole villages, or several villages, worked together to till the land now held in common.

The commune in China represents a new solution to the

In Sian, a photograph of youngsters spending the afternoons building sidewalks with their parents. But the grownups became silently and politely very angry with the photographer for they were sure he was photographing only the misery in their street, and considerable patience was needed to convince them that the sidewalk laying was the object of the pictures.

problem of growing enough food to feed the population in a large developing nation. It is radically different from the system of agriculture in most other Asian, African and Latin American countries, where private ownership of the land is still the rule. Through the commune, the peasant can pool his meager individual resources with others, enabling the communal group to buy tractors or large quantities of fertilizer which a single family would never be able to afford on its own. Most communes also have special shops to repair their own machinery, or factories to produce their own fertilizer. They share dairy herds, and maintain health clinics, athletic fields, and schools.

Communes also provide child care centers so that women are freed to take part in the work and the cultural and political activities of the community. By 1959, there were 4,980,000 such nurseries and kindergartens in China. They reflect a program of women's liberation in China which began with a new marriage law drafted the year after the Communists came to power. Article 9 read: "Both husband and wife shall have the right of free choice of occupation and free participation in work and social activities." This was a far cry from the position of women in traditional Chinese society. In the old days, a woman's parents selected her husband, and once married, she became little more than a convenient piece of furniture in her husband's house.

Since 1950, the Chinese have constantly sought to emphasize the new equality of women, encouraging them to work in jobs and positions not previously open to them. Women now manage factories, sit on the Central Committee of the Party and work in the fields. Recently, a Chinese ship with a woman captain and an all female crew called at the port of Vancouver, Canada. While a much-publicized railway is completely run and maintained by women.

Communes are able to organize large masses of people for public works: road and bridge-building, dams and irriga-

A woman factory worker, a common sight in Modern China.

tion ditches, or reforestation projects—planting trees on barren hillsides to prevent the soil from being washed away by wind and rain. As one peasant told the Swedish anthropologist, Jan Myrdal:

There was no mistrust of the people's commune among us. We considered it the only possibility. We had to develop our joint effort . . . Before, the masters had cave after cave of corn [in this particular section of China people lived in hillside caves], while the people went hungry. The people's commune was better, because it gave better possibilities for water regulation works and terracing of the hillsides, more order in planting our trees, more cultivation of vegetables and more odd jobs. We in Liu Ling Labour Brigade have managed to carry out big water regulation works and terracing thanks to the people's commune.

The Yellow River, once called "China's Sorrow" because of frequent floods which occurred when its muddy yellow waters overflowed their dikes, has now been tamed. In a massive plan to plant new trees, create reservoirs, and build over forty dams, some 6,600,000 acres of cultivable land were saved in an area where floods had killed millions of people over the past fifty years. The American writer Edgar Snow describes driving past the huge San Men dam on the Yellow River (which now generates some 1,200,000 kilowats of hydroelectricity yearly), and noticing how the river had changed since he had last seen it before the revolution:

As we came out of the pass we entered a plateau of beautiful farmlands and soon afterward reached a bluff where we stopped. Mr. Chin motioned me out [of the jeep] and led me to the precipice. A thousand feet below us, on either side of the wide new dam which had caught the Yellow River . . . lay a vast expanse of shimmering water as blue as the Aegean.

"Our yellow dragon has changed color," said Mr. Chin smiling. "He is tamed now."

Now, with flood and drought under control, better transportation of food from richer to poorer areas, and the equal distribution of food among the entire population, nobody starves to death in China.

Walk on Two Legs

This revolution in the villages of China is only part of the whole reorganization of Chinese society. The establishment of factories in the rural communes, for example, reverses the normal pattern of industrialization, in which industry is concentrated in the cities. In the West, in Russia, and in

Students building a sewer system.

most of the developing nations of the Third World, industries are built in and around major cities. This was also the case in China before the revolution. It led to the development of large industrial cities, especially in Manchuria and along the coast; Shanghai was the most famous of these cities. But of course, along with the growth of large urban areas came the problems of cities so familiar to Americans: pollution, slums, overcrowding and transportation problems. Furthermore, the Chinese realized that large factories concentrated in a few big cities would be highly vulnerable to air strikes. To avoid all these problems, the Chinese have dispersed their industry throughout the countryside. They are attempting to eliminate the usual gap between "modern" industrial cities and "backward" agricultural areas. As the Chinese repeatedly stress, China must "walk on two legs."

In a continuing effort to bridge the urban-rural gap, students and office workers from the city were sent to the countryside to work with the peasants in developing rural areas. Many were reluctant to leave the cities to do such menial labor, but Mao was insistent, viewing this limitation on individual freedom as an essential sacrifice which had to be made in order to build a new society where the old social distinctions would no longer exist. That students and bureaucrats should work with their hands and thus come in contact with the earth and the peasantry is only one part of a general ethic which seeks to prevent the growth of an intellectual elite divorced from the masses of China. Traditional Chinese philosophy had emphasized the distinction between scholars who labor with their minds and workers who labor with their bodies. It is a distinction which the Communists have relentlessly tried to break down in China.

There is probably no more consistent strain in the thought of Mao and the history of the Chinese revolution than the struggle against "elitism"—against the tendency of people in power to become arrogant, to regard themselves as superior to others, and to misuse their own power. As Mao wrote to Party leaders in 1949:

Guard against arrogance. For anyone in a leading position, this is a matter against principle and an important condition for maintaining unity. Even those who have made no serious mistakes and have achieved very great success in their work should not be arrogant.

The emphasis is on finding leadership which is responsive to the needs of the masses, and does not simply seek to increase its own power, prestige, or wealth.

A college dormitory scene. The revolution began with the struggle against the old
elite in China—the landlords in the villages, the capitalists
and corrupt officials in the cities. These were the men who
had oppressed the people in the past, collecting rents and
taxes from the peasantry while doing nothing in return,
and they were the first victims of the revolution. But someone had to run the factories, schools and government insti-
tutions of the new China created by the revolution. At first
the Chinese Communists followed the only example they had
—the Soviet Union—and in the early 1950's, technicians or
"experts" ran the factories, while professional teachers ran
the schools, generals ran the army, and Communist officials
ran the government. The Communist Party coordinated and
directed the whole effort.

But that did not end the problem of elitism. It simply replaced an elite of landlords, capitalists, and officials with an elite of Communists and "experts." In industry, the experts and engineers often insisted on running the factories as they saw fit, without listening to suggestions from workers. To Mao, who relied on the poor peasants to build his revolutionary movement and install a Communist government in China, it was an unacceptable way to run any enterprise. Mao had a deep faith in the ability of even the lowliest peasant to think problems through and solve them. At the same time, he had a deep distrust of men at the top, the so-called "experts," telling men at the bottom what to do and how to do it. If given a chance, the men at the top (who are always in the minority) would run things in their own interest, pretending to be working for all. And thus, for Mao, the problem of running a factory, an army, a commune or a school was not simply a question of finding new men for the top positions, but finding men who would not put themselves above those at the bottom. During the 1950s, the old experts in the factories were slowly replaced by "reds," or people who were able to understand that the object of factory production is not simply to create more goods, but to create goods which are needed by the majority and can be distributed equally.

For a time, that seemed to solve the problem. But by 1966, Mao began to feel that even the members of the Party had become an elite similar to the old landlords and capitalist factory managers who worked for their own profit before everything else. "With victory," Mao warned,

certain moods may grow within the Party—arrogance, the airs of a self-styled hero, inertia, unwillingness to make progress, love of pleasure and distaste for continued hard living . . . There may be some communists, who were not conquered by enemies with guns . . . but who can not withstand sugar-coated bullets.

An industrialist and his wife, who decided to stay when his factories were taken over by the state. He has added Mao's bust to the mantelpiece, and kept his comfortable house. He will receive five percent of the value of his factories as estimated by the government.

Throughout Mao's long career, he has frequently expressed fears that without struggle and a clear cause for which to sacrifice, revolutionary spirit would die and people would begin to grow soft and selfish long before revolutionary goals had been attained. Mao has always seen positive energy and value in struggle, which lies at the root of his whole dialectic view of the universe. It has been just this commitment to struggle and permanent revolution which has set the Chinese so against the Russians as revolutionary mentors. In the Chinese view, the Russians have long since sold out their revolution by allowing new inequalities to grow up in the form of privileges for Party officials. Fearing that the same phenomena had set in the Chinese Communist Party, Mao launched the Great Proletarian Cultural Revolution, a move which the Russians looked upon with complete disapproval.

The Cultural Revolution

It was a massive upheaval which puzzled most Westerners. China seemed to be attacking herself. The Communist Party was denounced by its own leaders as having become undemocratic, soft and self-seeking. One reads with amazement Mao's famous wall poster of 1966 called "Bombard the Headquarters." He was referring to the Party headquarters, and was calling on the Red Guards, composed mostly of high school and university students, to attack the Party which he himself had laboriously built up. The Party had grown old, rigid and timid. It was full of men who did not share Mao's sense of urgency and his belief that the revolution was far from being over. It is difficult to think of any other leader in the world who would have called on youth to "bombard" his own Kremlin, or White House, or House of Parliament, but Mao is not an ordinary political leader. He firmly believes that the new can flourish only after the old is dismantled and destroyed. As he wrote in a poem,

Since the thunderstorm has broken out over this earth
A spirit has emerged from a heap of skeletons.

Mao sees stability as leading to stagnation and elitism. Change is necessary. Old relationships must constantly be questioned. Old men out of step with the times must be replaced. Those in power must constantly be forced to "serve the people," or they must be removed from power.

During the Cultural Revolution, basic changes occurred in China. Political power was no longer the monopoly of the Communist Party as in the Soviet Union. Power was instead given to local Revolutionary Committees, composed of Party, army, peasant, worker and student representatives. Committees of workers, technicians, Party representatives and soldiers were established to run the factories.

Revolutionary changes also occurred in the schools and universities. In a country where before the revolution few peasants got any education at all, now over 90 percent of the youngsters in China at least attend primary school, and learn to read and write. The complex individual characters of the Chinese language have been simplified to make them easier to read. The object is to enable the people to read newspapers and books, so that literacy will not be confined to a privileged few. Yet during the Cultural Revolution it was discovered that in high schools and colleges, most of the students were the sons and daughters of the old upper classes, or the children of Communist Party members. Men in high positions in the Communist Party had begun to use their influence to ensure that their children got into the best schools and universities and received the best education. Peasants and workers were blocked from entering these schools by difficult entrance examinations.

Furthermore, much of the material taught in the schools was not relevant to the problems of the poor peasants and workers. An elite class continued to exist in the Chinese Communist education system. That elite was the target of the Cultural Revolution. As a result, most schools were completely shut down for over a year while the students struggled with teachers and principals, demanding that more peasants' and workers' sons and daughters be admitted, and demanding that teachers teach what the people need to learn.

Such criticism may not seem to justify closing down schools and universities all across the country. But to Mao, who had often referred to the outside world as the greatest classroom, the move made sense. Better that the schools be closed than have them teach irrelevant subjects to a privileged minority.

With attacks of this sort against "bourgeois" professors in the schools, and against "experts" in the factories, the Cultural Revolution proved a trying experience for the intellectuals of China. Accustomed to respect and favored treatment because of their greater education and knowledge, they found themselves forced to labor in the muddy rice paddies to learn the lot of the peasantry. And they were no longer free to teach what they wished, but had to follow the orders of people beneath them in learning.

Individual freedom has suffered during the Chinese revo-

告訴我們：要做一个有社会主义觉悟、有文化的劳动者·

Schoolchildren beside a portrait of Mao, talking to a group much like themselves. The slogan beneath the poster says: "Chairman Mao tells us that we must build a socialist consciousness and have literate workers."

lution. But if China had remained a nation of individuals, "a bowl of loose sand," as Sun Yat-sen called it, it would have remained a nation of disorganization, purposelessness and hunger. The freedom of the individual is seen as less important than the collective betterment of the Chinese people as a whole.

Criticism and self-criticism pervade Chinese society and grow directly from Mao's belief that it is healthy if an individual or a society is constantly moving and changing, and unhealthy if he or it is stagnant or resistant to change. He describes the role of self-criticism within the Chinese Communist Party:

Conscientious practice of self-criticism is still another hallmark distinguishing our Party from all other political parties. As we say, dust will accumulate if a room is not cleaned regularly; or faces will get dirty if they are not washed regularly. Our comrades' minds and our Party's work may also collect dust and also need sweeping and washing. The proverb, "Running water is never stale, and a door hinge is never worm-eaten" means that constant motion prevents the inroad of germs and other organisms.

Criticism meetings go on in China all the time. (The word *p'i p'ing*, to criticize, is one of the most common words in the Chinese language today.) These meetings might be described as political encounter groups of a sort. A peasant described one such meeting that took place in his own village:

After the winter harvest was in . . . there was less work in the fields. This was the time of year when life in the country quiets down and people occupy themselves with minor jobs. We then embarked on serious criticism and self-criticism. For months we kept at this and held discussions about it. We went through each one's faults and judged whether they had corrected them and how. We probed into ourselves and

examined each other and tried to get at the bottom of all our
personal problems, and each of our incorrect attitudes to life
and work. Sometimes, these meetings lasted half a day, and
we went on day after day. Altogether we had seventy or more
meetings. This meant that each of us in the group was
analyzed and corrected for anything up to fifty hours. Often
enough criticism hurt, but it helped . . . You know the old
person has to go, so that the new can emerge to take [his
or] her place.

The same techniques of group discussion and criticism are
used to reform criminals, and from all accounts, the results
seem to be impressive.

With this revolutionary approach of self-criticism, China
has made remarkable achievements in any number of fields.
She has transformed a country in which most of the people
could not read into one in which virtually all children attend
at least primary school. Tremendous strides have also been
made in the field of public health in China. Mass campaigns
have been organized to virtually eliminate disease-carrying
flies and snails. Diseases like tuberculosis, typhoid, cholera,
trachoma, and intestinal parasites, once common in China,
are now almost extinct. Health clinics exist in every community, and they are free. Venereal disease, once rampant
in the big cities, is no longer found in China at all. The
ability to organize the masses in tremendous public works
projects, often carried out through the communes, has allowed the Chinese to build roads, railroads, bridges, dams
and irrigation ditches throughout China. In the field of
science and technology, the Chinese have now built their
own nuclear weapons and orbited their own satellies around
the earth. These projects, while expensive, have given the
Chinese people a sense of strength and pride. For a nation
so often invaded, defeated, and humiliated, such achievements have had tremendous psychological as well as technical significance. China has now become truly a great power.

Such, then, are the broad outlines of the Chinese revolution. It is a revolution which has not always been easy to understand. At times China has seemed like a world apart from our own. But China's history and her problems were different from ours, and it should not be surprising that she finally chose solutions which were unfamiliar to us. While we stress stability and order in the United States, China devotes herself to self-criticism, struggle and revolutionary change. While we seek individual freedom and privacy, the Chinese stress organization and communality in service of the nation as a whole. As we become an increasingly urban country, living in cities and suburbs, China seeks to move people and industry out of the urban areas and into the countryside. While our educational system seeks to educate the best students and is designed to produce experts in various fields and vocations, Chinese education has tried to educate both the bottom and the top and to break down the mystique of the expert by forcing experts to become part of the common people. It reflects the Chinese Communist ideal that if the cities develop, so must the countryside; if industry is important, so is agriculture; if the brightest students are essential to China's future, so are the less fortunate and less educated; if the "experts" are crucial in solving China's problems, so are the common people.

The Chinese revolution is a new experiment without precedent in the history of the world. What China is doing in economic development, in education, and in social organization is totally different from what capitalist nations in the West, or communist nations like the Soviet Union, have tried before. To understand China is difficult enough. To evaluate it is nearly impossible. What we must realize, however, is that it is a new revolutionary society which we see in China, a society which deserves study, recognition and understanding. It is easy for people to say that because the Chinese experiment is so different, it must be evil, or doomed to failure. But if we wish to truly understand China, if we wish to really learn about China, we must try to develop an understanding of the Chinese revolutionary experience. Many of the problems they are struggling with are similar to our own. Perhaps they even have some answers which we ourselves have yet to discover. Perhaps. It is a possibility worth considering.

BIBLIOGRAPHY

The best single-volume general survey of Chinese society is John K. Fairbank, *The United States and China,* (Cambridge, Massachusetts: Harvard University Press, 1971). William Theodore de Bary et al., eds., *Sources of Chinese Tradition,* 2 volumes, (New York: Columbia University Press, 1960) contains translations of the basic writings of Chinese philosophy, religion and politics, and is especially valuable for the ancient period. A handy summary treatment of Chinese thought may be found in H. G. Creel, *Chinese Thought from Confucius to Mao Tse-tung,* (New York: Mentor, 1953). Franz Schurmann and Orville Schell, *The China Reader* (3 volumes), Volume 1: *Imperial China;* Volume 2: *Republican China;* and Volume 3: *Communist China,* (New York: Random House, 1967) contains a valuable selection of primary and secondary sources on China from the eighteenth century to the present day.

Two recent brief treatments of the Western impact on China are Wolfgang Franke, *China and the West: Cultural Encounter, 13th to 20th Centuries,* translated by R. A. Wilson, (New York: Harper and Row, 1967), and Pat Barr, *Foreign Devils: Westerners in the Far East, the Sixteenth Century to the Present Day,* (New York: Penguin Books, 1970), which is particularly valuable for its imaginative collection of illustrations. Johnathan Spence, *To Change China: Western Advisers in China 1620–1960,* (Boston: Little, Brown and Company, 1969) is an interesting collection of biographies of Westerners in China.

The May Fourth Movement as the beginning of the modern revolutionary era is given technical treatment in Chow Tse-tsung, *The May Fourth Movement, Intellectual Revolution in Modern China,* (Cambridge, Massachusetts: Harvard University Press, 1960). The 1920s are brilliantly described in Harold Isaacs, *The Tragedy of the Chinese Revolution,* (New York: Atheneum, 1966). Edgar Snow's *Red Star Over China,* (New York: Grove Press, 1961), has remained, since its first publication in 1938, the most vivid first-hand account of the Chinese Communist movement in the 1930s, and it contains an autobiography of Mao Tse-tung's early years as told to Snow in Yenan. An excellent recent biography of Mao is Stuart Schram's *Mao Tse-tung,* (New York: Pelican, 1968). Schram has also collected and translated many of Mao's most important writings in his *The Political Thought of Mao Tse-tung,* (New York: Praeger, 1963).

There are several first-hand accounts of China during World War II and the Civil War years of 1945–1949. One of the best is Annalee Jacoby and Theodore H. White, *Thunder Out of China,* (New York: Apollo, 1961). Jack Belden's *China Shakes the World,* (New York: Monthly Review Press, 1971) is particularly good on the Civil War period; and William Hinton's *Fanshen: A Documentary of Revolution in a Chinese Village,* (New York: Vintage, 1968) provides a vivid, detailed picture of revolution in one village. Barbara Tuchman's lengthy study, *Stillwell and the American Experience in China, 1911–1945,* (New York: Macmillan, 1970) provides a lively treatment of the American role in China during the twentieth century by focusing on a man who served as an ill-heeded advisor to Chiang Kai-shek during World War II.

On contemporary China, the third volume of the Schurmann and Schell *China Reader* (above) is an excellent collection of scholarly articles, eyewitness accounts and original source material. The best general account by a Western visitor to China is probably Edgar Snow's *Red China Today:*

The Other Side of the River, (New York: Vintage, 1971). *Report from a Chinese Village* by Swedish anthropologist Jan Myrdal, (New York: Signet, 1966), is a fascinating collection of peasants' accounts of life before and after the Revolution. There are at least two worthy accounts of the Cultural Revolution: Neale Hunter's *Shanghai Journal: An Eyewitness Account of the Cultural Revolution,* (New York: Praeger, 1969), and Gordon A. Bennet and Ronald N. Montaperto, *Red Guard: The Political Biography of Dai Hsiao-ai,* (New York: Doubleday, 1971). Finally, for a summary of the most recent events in China, see the collection of articles reprinted from the Bulletin of Atomic Scientists, *China After the Cultural Revolution,* D. Wilson and J. Simon, eds., (New York: Random House, 1969).

INDEX

About the Authors

Joseph Esherick studied as an under-graduate at Harvard University and did his graduate work at the University of California at Berkeley, where he received his Ph.D. from the department of history. He has traveled extensively in Asia and recently spent two years there on a Ford Foundation grant. He now teaches at the University of Oregon.

Orville Schell graduated from Harvard University and then spent two years in the Far East as a journalist and studying Chinese. He did his Ph.D. work at the Center for Chinese Studies at the University of California at Berkeley, and is presently co-director of the Bay Area Institute. He has written for *Look, Atlantic Monthly, The Nation, The New Republic, Saturday Review* and other publications. His books include THE CHINA READER and STARTING OVER.